Country Roads
~ of ~
KENTUCKY

A Guide Book
from Country Roads Press

Country Roads
~ of ~
KENTUCKY

Mary Augusta Rodgers

Illustrated by
Victoria Sheridan

Country Roads of Kentucky
© 1993 by Mary Augusta Rodgers. All rights reserved.

Published by Country Roads Press
P.O. Box 286, Lower Main Street
Castine, Maine 04421

Designed by Edith Allard.

Library of Congress Cataloging-in-Publication Data
Rodgers, Mary Augusta, 1922–
    Country Roads of Kentucky / Mary Augusta Rodgers :
[illustrated by] Victoria Sheridan.
      p. cm.
    Includes index.
    ISBN 1-56626-008-6 (pbk) : $9.95
      1. Kentucky—Tours. 2. Automobile travel—
Kentucky—Guidebooks.
  I. Title.
  F449.3.R63   1993
  917.690443—dc20   92-81832
                                       CIP

Printed in the United States of America.
10 9 8 7 6 5 4 3 2 1

To Hula and Andy Duke

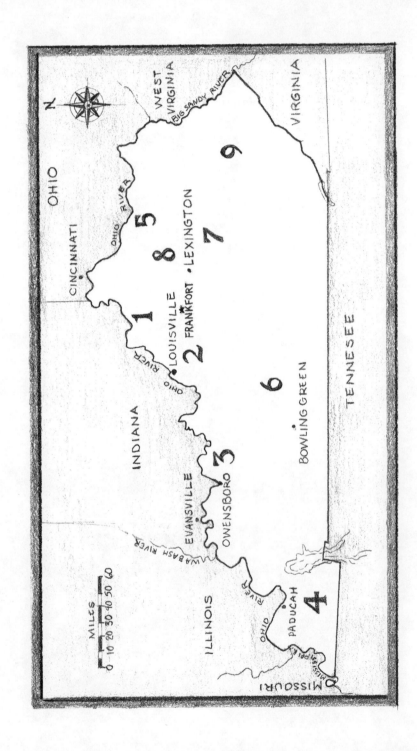

Contents

(& Key to Kentucky Country Roads)

Introduction   ix

1   North-Central Kentucky: Following the
     Ohio River   1

2   In and Around Louisville   9

3   Westward from Louisville Along the Ohio River   19

4   Southwest Kentucky: "The Purchase"   29

5   North-Central Kentucky to the
     Eastern Mountains   44

6   Driving Through the Cave Country   62

7   Easy-to-Reach Places off I-75   78

8   Following US 68: The Historic Buffalo Trace   92

9   Southeast Kentucky   117

     Epilogue: One Last Look   141

     Index   143

Introduction

Kentucky is my home state. I was born in Louisville, grew up there, and remain tied to Kentucky by a strong, invisible chain of memories and associations. Most of my adult life has been spent in Michigan. When we go back to Kentucky, we drive south through Ohio and cross the Ohio River at Cincinnati. I never see the "Welcome to Kentucky" sign without feeling a surge of emotion. Something happens to make the sky seem bluer, the trees greener, the road ahead more inviting. "And the birds make music all the day," in the words of Stephen Foster.

To be honest, I didn't have such strong feelings about Kentucky when I lived there. Louisville, in particular, was too close, too familiar, to be thought about or defined. I remember a friend saying impatiently, "How do I know what this town is like? It's home, that's all."

Home for me was Audubon Park, a Louisville suburb, where we lived on the corner of Cardinal Drive and Chickadee Road. And my idea of a country vista was the golf course across the street. Now Audubon Park is a tourist attraction during its two-day Dogwood Festival in April ("see beautifully illuminated trees and residents in antebellum costumes"). Antebellum? Well, I do declare!

Things change. Time and distance provide clarity and perspective. You see people and places better when they are not too close. Certainly that's been my experience, coming back to Kentucky as a visitor for many years.

Here's what I'd like to tell other visitors:

Kentucky is still a predominantly rural state. Louisville is the largest city, Lexington is second largest, Owensboro third. Perhaps no other state has little towns with such wild and wonderful names: Dwarf, Gravel Switch, Pippa Passes, Rabbit Hash, Sugartit, Turkey Neck Bend, and Hell-for-Certain, which may be spelled Hell-fer-Sartin.

Joe Creason, who wrote a Kentuckiana column in the *Louisville Courier-Journal*, always enjoyed these names. One of his reports: "James Still tells this story. . . . He was riding in an auto with several of his neighbors when they passed a sign saying 'Litter Barrel 1/2 Mile.' 'Well, dad-burn them highway people for always tinkerin' with the names of places,' one neighbor fumed. 'This place's been called Kellytown ever since I can rekerlect!' "

Kentucky is often called the Bluegrass State, a misleading term. The state can be divided most easily into four distinct areas: the north-central section, which includes the bluegrass country; the south-central, which includes the cave country; the eastern section, with the Appalachian Mountains; and the western section, with the Land Between the Lakes.

Traveling in Kentucky, you'll see miles and miles of beautiful country: from the white fences, black barns, and rich pastureland around Lexington to the mountains, deep gorges, and waterfalls in the eastern highlands; from the river towns along the banks of the Ohio to the cypress swamps near the Mississippi River. There are green hills and valleys, rocky cliffs, caves, forests; rivers, lakes, fast-flowing streams; and many small delights, like wild roses and mockingbirds, along the way.

In fact, Kentucky is an unusually scenic state, and due to a general lack of advertising billboards, so are its roads, expressways, and byways. You will see some man-made squalor here and there; consider it picturesque.

The climate? I'd say it's good. Spring is uncertain, rainy, and finally all flowers and fragrance. Summer is lush, hot, and languorous. Fall, my favorite season, is sunny and cool, with great bursts of red, yellow, rust, and gold from the trees. There's just enough winter to set the stage for spring: cold, dreary weather, interrupted now and then by snow, or an unexpected warm and sunny day.

The state has two time zones: most of north-central and all of eastern Kentucky are on Eastern time, while most of south-central and all of western Kentucky are on Central time. Or fast time and slow time, as many people say.

Kentuckians are unusually friendly and courteous people, when they are not surly and suspicious. They speak with a variety of accents: southern, midwestern, country, hard-to-place. Ask for directions in the mountains, and someone may say, "Hit's down the road a ways."

Ambiguities abound. This is the state that gave the country both Abraham Lincoln and Jefferson Davis (not to mention Carry A. Nation, who went around chopping up bars with an axe, and the mint julep). It's a border state, described as southern (my vote) or midwestern. Your impression will probably depend on where you are and the people you meet. Kentucky never seceded from the Union, but Kentuckians fought on both sides during the Civil War. The scars are growing faint, but they still show.

Famous for its tobacco, bourbon whiskey, and horse races, Kentucky is a state where many people strongly disapprove of all three. Consider that 76 of Kentucky's 120 counties are "dry," 30 are "wet," and 14 are "moist." Travelers who like a little bourbon and branch water before dinner should carry their own supplies.

Kentuckians love to tell stories. Often you can hear something—a rhythm, phrasing, a way with words—that suggests an oral tradition going back to frontier days. The storyteller starts a funny or outrageous story with a solemn expression, gives the audience a quick, sidelong glance at the midway point, and ends with a sudden roar of laughter. Mark Twain knew all about it.

Kentucky is an ideal state for country roads traveling, with its changing landscape, appealing little towns, and people who like to talk to strangers.

The state parks are excellent and well distributed throughout the state. Many offer comfortable lodge rooms, cottages—with kitchen, fireplaces, and cable TV—and campgrounds that are especially attractive in areas where other accommodations are limited. They make a good base for travelers who like to get out of their cars and explore the countryside. Now is the time, while rural and regional differences remain distinct. Signs of change are everywhere; consider the satellite dishes that sprout, like giant mushrooms, in the most remote areas.

Some of the nicest sights may not last much longer—ferries, for instance, and covered bridges, and band concerts in small town parks. Small towns could be on the endangered species list, the way things are going. They struggle with many problems—the competition from highway malls that drains their downtowns, to name one—and they do what they can. Greenville has a Washer Pitching Tournament in September, and Beattyville has a Woolly Worm Festival in October. Fulton, once the distribution center for most of the bananas imported into the United States, holds an International Banana Festival in late September that features a one-ton banana pudding.

Small towns have much to offer when you take the time. Pick a town that appeals to you, for one reason or another; perhaps Maysville, on the Ohio River, or Hazard in the mountains; Richmond, Princeton, Horse Cave, Henderson . . . the list could go on and on. Walk around for a while. Admire the courthouse or the town park. Pick out your favorite house. (My husband and I still remember a handsome 1810 brick house in Warsaw, restored and air-conditioned, with a sweeping view of the Ohio River, for sale at a reasonable price.)

Read the local newspaper. Don't skip the social column; it can give you a real feel for the town. Check out an antique shop or a yard sale. Have lunch at a local place.

We recall a late lunch in Perryville. It was after two in the afternoon, and the owner and his family were eating lunch themselves. Still, we were welcomed. "Arline can fix you something in no time," the owner said. "How about a fried chicken sandwich and iced tea?" "Honey, I was done eating, anyhow," Arline said, heading toward the kitchen. The others continued their conversation as they passed around a chocolate peanut butter pie. The talk was of politics, a nearby Japanese auto plant, unions, how to train hunting dogs, and we were invited to join in. It was a small place, unadorned except for a couple of wall calendars and sweet peas in jelly jars on the tables. We've seldom had such a pleasant time. The fried chicken sandwiches weren't bad, either. And the bill was $6.

This is not an all-inclusive guidebook, nor was it meant to be. Driving through Kentucky, we followed our own interests and inclinations, and trust that readers will do the same, trying some of the numbered tours and using others as a starting point to create their own itineraries "to taste."

To simplify road designations, I've used the following abbreviations: I = Interstate; US = U.S. Route or Highway; KY = State Route or Highway.

I wish I could thank everyone who helped out along the way. Special thanks and affection go to Dottie Harris and Mary Vaughan in Louisville, and Hula and Andy Duke in Maysville. In many ways, this book is a joint venture. Bill and I traveled together; I took notes, he took photographs. We didn't always agree. (He likes caves, I don't. He gets bored with historical markers, I never do.) Still, we very much enjoyed our travels in Kentucky. We hope you will, too.

Country Roads
~ of ~
KENTUCKY

1 ~

North-Central Kentucky:

Following the Ohio River

Take I-75 south from Cincinnati to US 42 south to KY 338 west.

Highlights: *Old river towns, historic houses, General Butler State Resort Park, and a war story about Warsaw, Kentucky.*

Once, frontier scouts and early settlers reached Kentucky by coming down the Ohio in canoes or on flatboats—a long and dangerous trip. Now travelers driving south on I-75 leave downtown Cincinnati, cross the Ohio River, and pass the church spires and hills of Covington, Kentucky, all in a matter of minutes. While crossing the Ohio, you might take a look at the second bridge on your left, a suspension bridge built in 1866 by John Roebling, who went on to build a similar structure, the Brooklyn Bridge, in New York City.

The trip from Big Bone Lick State Park to Louisville is about 130 miles long. Head south on I-75 from Cincinnati. Note that the greater Cincinnati International Airport is located in Kentucky's Boone County. The usual clusters of motels and chain restaurants appear on the way to Florence, including a Tudor castle–type motel called the Drawbridge Inn (505 units), which looks larger than many towns. Leave I-75 at Florence; take US 42 south. Here the road goes southwest and the countryside soon turns rural; you'll see some horse farms with their green pastureland and white fences, and a sign announcing the Ohio River Beagle Club. Take KY 338 west.

This leads to Big Bone Lick State Park; the name essentially tells the story. In prehistoric times, sulphur springs and salt licks drew herds of giant mastodons, mammoths, and bison to this valley. Many of them sank and died in the surrounding marshes, where their bones were preserved. A Virginian who reached the valley in 1773 found the ground covered with huge bones; he and his party used mastodon ribs for tent poles, vertebrae for seats, and carried ten-pound teeth home for souvenirs. In 1805, Thomas Jefferson sent a group to collect bones. Other collectors followed until the bones were all gone. (Some are now displayed in American and European museums.) The park maintains a herd of buffalo and displays models of prehistoric mastodons and bison along the trail that leads to the remaining springs. You'll find a lake and a well-equipped campground here as well.

Suggested side trip: Continue west on KY 338, nine miles to Rabbit Hash, a nineteenth-century village just across the river from Rising Sun, Indiana. The action, if any, is at the general store. Rabbit Hash has had a store since 1831, but the present structure was built in 1919 and is on the National Register of Historic Places. What do you do in Rabbit Hash?

*On the National Register of Historic Places, the Rabbit Hash
General Store has been serving customers since 1919*

Most visitors buy postcards, or something marked with the
town's name—an apron proclaiming the Rabbit Hash Gourmet
Cooking School, for instance. Or you could buy the town; it's
been advertised for sale—3.7 acres including the general
store, an old barn, a blacksmith shop, a few log cabins, and a
rusty mailbox—for $639,500 in *Historic Preservation News*.

There are several stories explaining the name. One dates from 1816, when a flood drove thousands of rabbits into the surrounding hills. "Anything to eat around here?" one traveler asked another. The reply was, "Plenty of rabbit hash!"

Go east on KY 338 to US 42, then south on US 42. You travel through hills and valleys, deep green woods, past an old barn with a "Chew Mail Pouch" sign and other signs advertising "Live Bait." This is fine fishing country. The Ohio River comes into view near Paint Lick, a stream converted into a lake by the Markland Dam, and stays close all the way to General Butler State Resort Park. You see a "Congested Area" sign and an empty road beyond, and then Warsaw appears—an old river town with the chalk-white Gallatin County Courthouse as its focal point. Seven American flags stand at attention on the balcony, one for each of the Warsaw-area men who served in the Desert Storm operation and returned home safely. The significance of the flags was explained by a man in jogging shorts who turned out to be Gallatin County's presiding judge. He also told us that the original courthouse, built in 1838, had a bell tower that was eliminated in 1939, when the building was remodeled. "But they kept the old bell. It's still up there in the attic."

Warsaw has an in-town cornfield and tobacco patch. Houses on West High Street keep their backs to the river view, a result of the terrible 1937 flood, during which most of the existing houses were swept away. So many people were left homeless that the Red Cross came in and built a row of houses. "They're still here, on Red Cross Avenue, and folks still living in them."

Next comes Ghent, first known, more inelegantly, as Mc-Cool's Creek—a town of handsome old houses and beautiful river views. The Ghent House Bed & Breakfast Inn, built in 1833, is an attractive establishment with a rose garden in back and a river view.

Then you reach Carrollton, the county seat of Carroll County and "the second largest burley tobacco market in the world." Another of Joe Creason's Kentucky stories: "Early in World War II, just after Hitler invaded Poland, a man came running into a Carrollton hardware store and asked for all the shotgun shells on hand. Why all the ammunition? 'I just heard on the radio that the Germans are in Warsaw,' he cried, out of breath. 'But they'll get a hell of a fight from me if they try to take Carrollton!' "

General Butler State Resort Park, just outside Carrollton, is an example of Kentucky's excellent park system. (The term "resort park" indicates that the park has a lodge and a restaurant.) Butler has pleasant cottages, good camping sites, a lake, a pool, golf, and tennis, all in a secluded setting of hills, woodlands, and river views. Early in May, the park rings with the sound of bagpipes as the Kentucky Scottish Weekend is celebrated with Scottish music, food, dance, and athletic competitions. "Ski Butler!" reads one sign, promising twenty acres of ski trails in the winter and "one of the most advanced snow-making systems available." (In Kentucky, they need it.)

The park was developed by the Civilian Conservation Corps in the early 1930s. In 1939, admission was 10 cents, overnight camping 25 cents, and a furnished cabin cost $2.00 a night. A dramatic view of the Ohio River valley dominates the lodge. Lookout Point offers a good view of the confluence of the Kentucky and Ohio rivers.

Also on the park grounds you'll find the 1859 Butler-Turpin House. General Thomas Butler, for whom the park is named, was an aide to Andrew Jackson at the Battle of New Orleans. There were five Butler brothers, all military men. "When I wanted a thing well done, I ordered a Butler to do it," General Lafayette said. Simple yet impressive, the house is furnished with some original pieces. A dogtrot leads to the separate kitchen which is made homey by a loaf of bread, biscuits, and a cherry pie, all of stone. (The stony biscuits looked all too familiar; I've tried them when they were called "beaten biscuits.")

Two miles north of Carrollton, on US 42, you'll find the 1790 Masterson House, one of the oldest brick houses left along the Ohio River. While the Mastersons lived there, it also served as a Methodist church and as the county's first courthouse. Sarah and Richard Masterson, the original owners, are buried on the grounds. The setting is quiet and, by now, suburban. At the house next door, a man was mowing the grass while a beagle puppy chased a white kitten around the garage.

Carrollton, founded in 1794, could serve as a model for other river towns, with its courthouse square, drowsy downtown, and handsome old houses lining shady streets. The historic district includes the 1825 house built for General William Butler and the restored 1812 Carrollton Inn, with ten rooms and a restaurant. Maps of the historic district are available at the Old Stone Jail, now a Visitors Information Center.

Carrollton today is quiet and charming. But like other river towns, it has a rough and rowdy past. In the days when the Ohio River was Kentucky's main highway and steamboats made regular runs, Carrollton was a wide-open town. Landing docks, warehouses, wagons, and taverns full of card sharks and prostitutes kept the waterfront lively day and night. Drunken brawls were a regular amusement among the rivermen. The legendary Mike Finn, "king of the keel-boaters," expressed the spirit of the times: "I can hit like fourth-proof lightnin' and every lick lets in an acre of sunshine. I can out-run, out-jump, out-shoot, out-brag, out-drink, and out-fight any man on both sides of the river!"

South of Carrollton, US 42 crosses the Kentucky River. Just past the bridge, take US 36 west. The road follows the Ohio River to Milton through green hills and pastoral valleys, the river appearing and disappearing among the trees.

At a stop near Milton, we met an energetic woman out for her morning walk with hand weights and a Walkman. She said she lived across the road. Having just admired the house, I asked if it was very old. "Oh, yes!" she said. "Built in the 1930s." In an engaging rush, she told us about her husband's illness, surgery, and recent recovery, her sons' college choices and preference in football teams, where to buy the best peaches, and why she'd grown to hate tobacco. "Some people around here feel the same way," she said. "They're growing soybeans instead."

Following her advice, we drove through Milton, with a brief stop to admire the large boat dock and a bridge across the Ohio to Madison, Indiana. Near the boat dock was a ramshackle building marked "Milton Boat Club."

Past Milton take KY 421 south. As instructed, we stopped at the first farmer's stand. The peaches were luscious. Then we followed the winding road past Bedford, the county seat of Trimble County, through farm country and a violent thunderstorm to I-71 and on to Louisville.

In the Area

Big Bone Lick State Park, 3380 Beaver Rd., Union, KY 41091; 606-384-3522.

Ghent Bed & Breakfast Inn, 411 Main Street, US 42. 502-347-5807 (weekends); 606-291-0168 (weekdays).

General Butler State Resort Park, Box 325, Carrollton, KY
41008-0325; 502-732-4384 or 1-800-325-0078.

Masterson House, US 42 N. Open Sunday, 2:00-5:00 p.m.;
Memorial Day to Labor Day. 502-732-8204.

Carrollton Tourist Commission, P.O. Box 293, Carrollton, KY
41008; 502-732-7036 or 1-800-325-4290.

Carrollton Inn, 218 Main St., off US 42. 502-732-6905.

2 ~

In and Around Louisville

Take I-75 to Louisville.

Highlights: *Big events (the Derby, the Humana Festival, etc.), nice little surprises (ice cream, Tarzan memorabilia, etc.), good food and drink, interesting architecture, and more.*

Louisville is not only the largest of Kentucky's river towns, it's one of the oldest, founded by George Rogers Clark in 1778, its town charter signed by Thomas Jefferson, then governor of Virginia, in 1780. Through the years, it's had many illustrious visitors, including Charles Dickens in 1842, who liked the town but complained about pigs in the streets. Like all successful tourist towns, the name Louisville is associated with good times; people think of horse races, mint juleps, baseball bats, Kentucky colonels, and southern belles. It's all still there—plus a great deal more—although the Kentucky colonels and southern belles are increasingly over-age and out of date.

9

Mention Louisville and everyone thinks horse racing

Not too long ago, Louisville was essentially an overgrown small town known as "the gateway to the South." Now it's a real city ringed by expressways, with a skyline and a formerly neglected waterfront as its showplace. But many southern small-town airs and graces remain.

Louisville is an easy place for visitors to deal with. There are a number of good restaurants and hotels to choose from, but not so many that the choice becomes bewildering. Finding your way around is easy, and distances are not great. In the summer, the city is green with trees and parks; there's more parkland per person here than in any other city in the country.

Be prepared for some surprises. Most visitors, who know about Derby Day and the attendant festivities and little else, miss out on the rich assortment of plays, concerts, ballet performances, and other events provided by Louisville's thriving cultural community. Check to see what's on at the Actors Theater of Louisville, the Kentucky Center for the Arts, the Louisville Ballet, the Louisville Orchestra, and the Louisville Bach Society.

By now it's generally known that Hillerich & Bradsby's Louisville Slugger bat factory is actually across the river in Jeffersonville, Indiana. But did you know that one of the world's best-known songs, "Happy Birthday to You," was written in Louisville in 1893? Or that the J. B. Speed Museum has the world's greatest collection of Tarzan and Edgar Rice Burroughs manuscripts and material?

Here are some suggestions for a do-it-yourself tour that includes both main and side-street attractions. Start at the Riverfront Plaza and Belvedere on the Ohio River at Fifth and Main streets; an eight-acre landscaped overlook with a water garden, a bronze statue of George Rogers Clark, and a wharf where the stern-wheeler, the *Louisville Belle,* waits between cruises. The statue is significant. General Clark is pointing forward and looking back, like Louisville, a city old and new, turning back to the river where it all began. On a good day the views—of the river, the Falls Fountain to the east, the Falls of the Ohio to the northwest, Indiana to the west—are great.

Lodgings

The Brown Hotel, at Fourth Avenue and Broadway, is a Louisville institution, now restored to its former glory. President Herbert Hoover was a guest at the Brown during the week of the great stock market crash in 1929. A fish was caught in the lobby during the 1937 flood, and a baby was born on the seventeenth floor. The Hot Brown sandwich, a satisfying luncheon dish made with toasted bread, sliced breast of chicken, a rich cheese sauce, and a strip of bacon, was invented here. (Not as well known is the Cold Brown: rye bread, Bibb lettuce, sliced breast of chicken, a slice of tomato, and Thousand Island dressing over all.)

The Seelbach Hotel, on Fourth Avenue, is another Louisville landmark, built in 1905 and full of *belle époque* elegance. You enter a lobby of marble, bronze, and mahogany with a curving stairway, crystal chandeliers, and a domed ceiling of beveled glass. William Howard Taft, Woodrow Wilson, Isadora Duncan, and John F. Kennedy were among the distinguished guests here. Daisy Buchanan, the beautiful heroine of F. Scott Fitzgerald's novel *The Great Gatsby*, once danced the night away at the Seelbach. It's still her kind of place.

The Old Louisville Inn Bed & Breakfast, on Third Street, was built in 1901 as the home of the president of the Louisville Home Telephone Company, a man who evidently liked some pomp and circumstance. The house has mahogany woodwork, ornate carved mahogany columns in the lobby, twelve-foot ceilings painted with murals, baronial marble bathrooms, and many fireplaces. The Inn's eleven bedrooms are nicely furnished, with antique quilts on the beds, and feature a number of thoughtful touches, like a selection of books and notepaper with stamped envelopes. Hot popovers are a breakfast speciality, along with muffins, fresh fruit, and homemade granola, and you can eat at a table in the back courtyard when the weather's right.

Sights and Shopping

Sightseeing in and around the downtown Louisville area begins at the Filson Club, South Third Street, a museum whose collections reflect Kentucky history: portraits, maps, guns, Shaker pieces, and a tree stump with the inscription "D. Boon Kil A Bar 1803."

Much of Louisville's history is evident in its architecture, a rich mix that should include the many rows of two-story houses of dark red brick with white trim that remain in the city. (Seldom mentioned, they still mean Louisville to me.) Belgravia and St. James courts, the heart of the Old Louisville historic district, include some wonderfully showy Victorian mansions of stone and brick. The Conrad-Caldwell House, in St. James Court, has a hand-carved marble façade complete with gargoyles, stained glass windows, and period furniture, and is open for tours.

The Pendennis Club, another noteworthy Louisville institution, stands on the corner of Third Street and Muhammed Ali Boulevard, formerly Chestnut Street. Mixologists, take note: the old-fashioned cocktail was invented at the Pendennis. The Jefferson County Courthouse, on West Jefferson, is considered an outstanding example of Greek Revival architecture. Designed in 1835, completed in 1850, its massive size and grand design reflect the fact that it was meant to be the state capitol building; many people thought at the time that Louisville would become the state capital. But Frankfort held firm.

Main Street, dreary and neglected for many years, has become a busy, stylish street full of striking buildings. Visitors are usually surprised to see so many classic cast-iron buildings of the late 1800s on Main Street; only New York City's Soho district has more. A good example is the building occupied by the Museum of History and Science. For contrast there's the postmodern Humana Building, designed by Michael Graves, at Fifth and Main, the Mies van der Rohe American Life Building, and the contemporary Kentucky Center for the Arts. The famed Actors Theater of Louisville occupies an 1857 Greek Revival building.

The Kentucky Art and Crafts Gallery, on Main Street, has an outstanding selection of contemporary art and craft pieces that includes wearable art and jewelry, clothing, toys, pottery, and sculpture. From Main Street it's not far to Joe Ley Antiques, on East Market Street, which does business in an 1890 three-story brick schoolhouse enclosed by a high iron fence. Behind the fence, the grounds are bursting with all kinds of outdoor furniture, lights, and ornaments: elaborate fountains and birdbaths, statues of demure Grecian maidens and stalwart men, stone bunnies, cast-iron deer, hitching-post jockeys, and so on. Inside, you'll find all the usual antique items as well as carousel horses, mahogany mantels, beveled glass fanlights, 5,000 doors, player pianos. . . . It would be easier to list what Joe Ley's *doesn't* have.

Another shopping note: Bardstown Road, from Baxter Avenue to the Douglas loop, is a good area for antique shops, art galleries, restaurants, and speciality stores such as The Doll Collection. So is Frankfort Avenue in the Crescent Hill section of town, from Mellwood Road to Stilz.

Dining Out

Restaurants in Louisville moved well beyond such fare as fried chicken, country ham, and beaten biscuits years ago. Traditional dishes like chicken hash, cheese grits, chess pie, and Benedictine sandwiches are still around, but often appear in new versions. The Hot Brown becomes an omelet, for instance, and the Benedictine filling (cream cheese flavored with cucumber and spring onions) is served on endive leaves as an hors d'oeuvre.

Kaelin's restaurant, on Newburg Road, claims to have served the country's first cheeseburger in 1934. They're still at it. Other old-time Louisville establishments include Kunz's Fourth & Market and Jack Fry's on Bardstown Road. The Rudyard Kipling, on Oak Street, is a restaurant, bar, and popular hang-out. The eclectic menu includes Cornish pasties and Kentucky burgoo, and there's entertainment six nights a week upstairs. "One night they'll have a band from Ireland and the next night a playwright trying out a new play."

Any list of Louisville's best restaurants would be likely to include Dietrich's in the Crescent (a bistro menu, open kitchen, wood-burning grill), La Paloma (dishes from Spain, Italy, Greece, Morocco), Lilly's (Continental, with a seasonal Kentucky flavor), and Vincenzo's (elegant Italian).

In a class by itself is the Afro-German Tea Room, behind St. Martin's Church, Shelby and Gray streets, a cozy place with excellent food and some volunteer waitresses. (The name reflects the neighborhood's ethnic history, not the style of cooking.) Profits go to benefit the Urban Montessori Schools.

Erhmann's Bakery, in the Mid-City Mall on Bardstown Road, has the best ice cream in the state (I'm restraining myself; in the country, I'd like to say.) Try the chocolate and vanilla in combination, or the caramel, or an ice cream cake known as "Cupid's Delight." They serve a mean chocolate soda, too. The ambiance is, well, mid-city mall, but Erhmann's old soda fountain, moved from their original location, is a treasure, with a marble counter, marble columns, a stained glass border, and a back mirror.

Parks

Louisville's parks offer some surprising features as well as golf courses, tennis courts, pools, exercise tracks, stables, and fishing lakes. Seneca Park, for instance, has a Braille Trail nature walk. Central Park is the setting for the Kentucky Shakespeare Festival, one of only three independent, professional, and free Shakespeare festivals in the country, offering outdoor performances from June through August. (The 1992 season included *Much Ado About Nothing* and *Othello.*) A park named for Joe Creason, the late *Louisville Courier Journal* Kentuckiana columnist, is on Trevilian Way, near the Louisville Zoo. Cherokee Park, guarded by a dignified statue of Daniel Boone, is my favorite of Louisville's many fine parks; it borders a Historic Preservation District of fine old houses now known as the Cherokee Triangle.

Cave Hill Cemetery, on Baxter Avenue, is a peaceful 300-acre retreat, with splendid old trees, ponds with swans, lakes, even a cave, and paths winding among the graves of the known and the unknown. General George Rogers Clark and Colonel Harlan Sanders are buried here, along with 5,000 or so Civil War soldiers.

The River Road and Water Tower area was described by *Courier Journal* reporter Bob Hill as a "flowing blend of river, trees, farmland, public parks, old money, new money, no money, and a golf driving range."

Special Events

Heading the list is the Kentucky Derby, accompanied by several weeks of organized uproar beginning in mid-April and lasting until Derby Day, the first Saturday in May. The Derby Festival begins in April with "Thunder Over Louisville," a display of fireworks said to be "the greatest fireworks show *anywhere.*"

The Humana Festival of New American Plays, held from late February through March at the Actors Theater, is a showcase for new and established playwrights. If you want tickets for the opening weekend, when theater critics come in from all over the country, write or call the Actors Theater a year ahead. (Tickets for later dates are not as hard to get.)

The Hard Scuffle Steeplechase (fourth Saturday in May, at the Hard Scuffle Farm in nearby Prospect) is becoming known as Louisville's second Derby Day. "And one more chance to wear those beautiful garden-party hats."

The Louisville City Fair (mid-June, Riverfront Plaza and Belvedere) is a two-day celebration of Louisville neighborhoods set to music from bluegrass to blues and jazz.

The Corn Island Storytelling Festival (mid-September) features storytellers from all over on the *Belle of Louisville* stern-wheeler as it steams down the Ohio, and at other city locations.

Dickens on Main Street takes place on November 27 in connection with Light Up Louisville, when the downtown holiday lights go on. Roasted chestnuts and other seasonal treats, music and exhibits of the Dickens era; Victorian costumes are encouraged. "We can't count on snow, unfortunately, but when it does, the effect is magical."

In the Area

All telephone numbers are within area code 502.

Actors Theater of Louisville, 316 W. Main St. Tours. 584-1265. Box office: 584-1205.

Kentucky Center for the Arts, 5 Riverfront Plaza. 584-7777 or 1-800-775-7777.

Louisville Ballet, 1300 Bardstown Rd. 456-4527.

Louisville Orchestra, 609 W. Main St. 587-8681.

Louisville Bach Society, 4607 Hanford Lane. 585-2224.

J. B. Speed Museum, 2035 S. Third St. 636-2893. Open Tuesday through Saturday, 10:00 a.m.-4:00 p.m.; closed Mondays and holidays.

The Belle of Louisville, Fourth Ave. and River Rd. Excursions run Memorial Day through Labor Day, 2:00 p.m. daily except Monday. Sunset cruises sail Tuesday and Thursday, 7:00-9:00 p.m. 625-2355.

The Brown Hotel, Fourth Ave. and Broadway. 1-800-866-7666 or 583-1234.

The Seelbach Hotel, 500 Fourth Ave. 1-800-333-3349 or 585-3200.

The Old Louisville Inn, 1359 S. Third St. 635-1574.

The Filson Club, 1310 S. Third St. 635-5083. Open Monday through Friday, 10:00 a.m.-4:00 p.m.; Saturday, 9:00 a.m.-noon.

Belgravia and St. James Courts, between Breckinridge and Ninth St., just off Central Park.

Old Louisville Information Center, in Central Park, has walking maps.

Conrad-Caldwell House, 1402 St. James Ct. 636-5023. Tours Monday through Wednesday, 1:00-5:00 p.m.; Sunday, 1:00-5:00 p.m.

Jefferson County Courthouse, 531 W. Jefferson. 625-5761.

Museum of History and Science, 727 W. Main St. 561-6103. Has an IMAX theater. Open daily.

Kentucky Art and Craft Gallery, 609 W. Main St. 589-0102. Open Monday through Saturday, 10:00 a.m.-4:00 p.m..

Joe Ley Antiques, 615 E. Market St. 583-4014. Open Tuesday through Saturday, 8:30 a.m.-5:00 p.m.

Kaelin's, 1801 Newburg Rd. 451-1801.

Kunz's Fourth and Market, 115 Fourth Ave. 585-5555.

Jack Fry's, 1007 Bardstown Rd. 452-9244.

The Rudyard Kipling, 422 W. Oak St. 636-1311

Dietrich's in the Crescent, 2862 Frankfort Ave. 897-6076.

La Paloma, 3612 Brownsboro Rd. 895-5493.

Lilly's, 1147 Bardstown Rd. 451-0447.

Vincenzo's, Humana Conference Center, 150 S. Fifth St. 580-1350.

Afro-German Tea Room, Shelby & Gray sts. 585-3484. Lunch served 11:00 a.m.-2:00 p.m., Monday through Friday. Dinner by reservation, Friday and Saturday.

Ehrmann's Bakery, 1250 Bardstown Rd. 451-6720.

Cherokee Park, junction of Eastern Parkway and Cherokee Parkway.

Louisville and Jefferson County Metro Parks. 456-8100.

Cave Hill Cemetery, 701 Baxter Ave. Open daily, 8:00 a.m.-4:45 p.m.

3 ~

Westward from Louisville Along the Ohio River

Take US 31W and US 60 south from Louisville to KY 1638 west.

Highlights: *The Doe Run Inn, more old river towns and historic houses, Audubon State Park, Henderson, a quilt museum, plus Lincoln stories and a mention of Madonna.*

From the Gold Depository at Fort Knox to Paducah is a trip of about 272 miles. Take US 31W and US 60 south from Louisville. US 31W goes through a heavily commercial area, then passes West Point and the Fort Knox Military Reservation, where the Patton Museum of Cavalry and Armor and the Gold Depository are located. Take the Chaffee Avenue exit off US 31W to the Patton Museum. Military history buffs will enjoy cavalry and armor exhibits, the personal effects of General George S. Patton, and the military history library.

Gold Vault Road leads to the Gold Depository, home of most of the U.S. gold reserve. There is no admittance, but you can gaze at the granite, steel, and concrete building from the road and take a few shots . . . *snapshots*, that is. It's not an inspiring sight.

At Muldraugh, take KY 1638 west. This route leads to Otter Creek Park, located thirty miles from Louisville on the site of Rock Haven, a town that was destroyed in the 1937 flood. The 3,000-acre park is scenic, with steep cliffs and heavily wooded banks along the Ohio River. Otter Creek is a small deep stream.

Turn left on KY 448 to Doe Run Creek and the Doe Run Inn. Some famous names are connected with this lovely little creek, flowing over limestone through the trees, and the stone building that stands nearby. Squire Boone, Daniel's brother found the creek, named it, and later claimed title to the land; the deed was signed by Patrick Henry, governor of Virginia. In 1816, construction began on the building. The limestone walls were built two feet thick and the timbers were hand hewn of black walnut. According to an old record book, Abraham Lincoln's father was employed as a stone mason at the site.

On a hot summer day, the Doe Run Inn looked just right for a country weekend: cool, shady, far away. It's hard to realize you're only thirty-eight miles from Louisville. The inn's bedrooms are furnished with antiques, a gift shop is stocked with locally made quilts, and the dining room was serving a Friday night special: barbecued pork, three vegetables, and dessert for $6.95.

Take KY 448 north to KY 1638 west to Brandenburg. Brandenburg's Main Street runs to the Ohio River, an arrangement that encouraged trade and riverboat stops—and some hard-to-handle visitors like John Hunt Morgan, the Confederate raider, and Jesse James. The town was named for

Colonel Solomon Brandenburg, an early settler who served in the War of 1812. In 1855, another veteran of that war, Colonel Buckner, built a hillside house with a panoramic view of the Ohio River. During the Civil War, the house, then known as the Buckner Homestead, was used as a command post by Colonel Morgan as he ferried his Confederate troops across the Ohio on captured steamboats. The house still stands, and the view is still spectacular. It's worth a look. Find Lawrence Road, near the river, and watch for the historical marker. You'll see a white house with an unusually wide and elegant doorway, an official Historic Place, with a child's swing set in the yard and laundry on the line, the day we were there.

We were advised to stay on Lawrence Road, which quickly becomes Battle Road, to Wolf Creek. "If you like scenic drives," a Brandenburg man said, "that's a real good one." He was right.

Suggested side trip: Take KY 228 (Battle Road) north to Wolf Creek. The road then loops south through several small towns to KY 79 near Brandenburg.

Take KY 79 South to US 60. This leads to Hardinsburg, Cloverport, and Hawesville. Hardinsburg, a small farming community, is known nationwide for the fine needlework done by local farm women. Since 1929, local seamstresses have turned out smocked and beribboned baby dresses, mono-grammed linens, and luxurious items like quilted satin robes and lingerie cases, which are sold in shops such as Saks Fifth Avenue and Neiman Marcus. One source of this finery, the Galante Studio on Main Street, is Hardinsburg's largest em-ployer; the next largest is the Eleanor Beard Studio, also on Main. We were in Hardinsburg late on a hot afternoon and found the Eleanor Beard shop closed; the window displayed some decorative pillows, a quilted bed jacket, and a sign that read "Free Scraps."

Continuing west on US 60, the drive from Hardinsburg to Cloverport is lovely, winding through hilly countryside. You see farms, ponds, and black barns, green hills and valleys, and finally the Ohio River shining in the sun. Cloverport is another nice little river town. The houses here bravely face the water. There's some historical evidence that Thomas Lincoln, his wife, and their two young children crossed the Ohio near Cloverport on their way to Indiana in 1816. They had a yoke of oxen hitched to a cart and a cow. According to one report, the children looked hungry. It's a poignant picture. But you wonder why the Lincolns, one of many pioneer families moving west at the time, attracted such attention; Abraham Lincoln was then five years old.

Just east of Hawesville, there's a good view of the Ohio and the Lincoln Trail Bridge to Cannelton, Indiana. And another Lincoln story: Abe Lincoln was eighteen and working on a ferry just south of Hawesville, when, on his own time, he rowed two men out to a steamboat and was paid 50 cents by each man. The ferry owner sued, claiming "infringement of ferry privileges." Lincoln defended himself on the grounds that he hadn't taken the men *across* the river, but only halfway, and was acquitted. The Squire Pate House, built of logs in 1822, was the scene of the trial, with Squire Pate presiding; you can find it past Hawesville, just off KY 334, four miles east of Lewisport. Hawesville is the county seat of Hancock County.

Route 60, from the Hancock County line to Owensboro, is named the Josiah Henson Trail in honor of a slave who might have been the inspiration for Uncle Tom in Harriet Beecher Stowe's *Uncle Tom's Cabin*. ("So you're the little lady who started this big war," President Lincoln said, on meeting Mrs. Stowe.) Josiah Henson was in any case a remarkable man. A slave on the Reilly plantation near Owensboro, he became a Methodist minister, tried to buy his freedom, and finally fled to Canada with his wife and four children. US 60 connects with the Audubon Parkway, which loops around Owensboro—Kentucky's third largest city, home of Bar-B-Q, bluegrass music, and the blues—and goes on to Henderson.

Take US 41 north to the John James Audubon State Park. Henderson was the only dry town between Point Pleasant, West Virginia, and Cairo, Illinois, during the 1937 flood. Hence its slogan: "Henderson: On the river but never in it." The town's most famous resident was a man named John James Audubon, who lived in a log house near the corner of Main and Second streets from 1810 to 1819 and failed at running a gristmill and a general store. The land where Audubon spent much of his time, observing and sketching birds, is now part of the John James Audubon State Park in Henderson. The woods and meadows are beautiful, full of wildflowers in the spring, and on the route for many migratory birds . . . as well as that well-known species, the Avid Rosy-Faced Birdwatcher. Audubon Park has a nature preserve lake, more than five miles of hiking trails, fishing, golf, tennis, cottages, and campsites. The John James Audubon Museum, on the park grounds, has been closed for renovation but will open in late 1993 to display its famous collection of Audubon's work. Meanwhile, it's hard to miss the building, which resembles a French chateau, with a tower used by nesting birds.

Henderson's Welcome Center for visitors is on US 41 north, across the street from the entrance to the park. We stopped by, and were given a walking map of Henderson— "We've kept our downtown and that makes *all* the difference!"—and advice on the best place for barbecue: Thomason's, on Atkinson Street. "It's just an itty, bitty, dinky place, but you'll love it."

Audubon isn't Henderson's only famous name. W. C. Handy, who wrote "St. Louis Blues," was born here. So was Mary Towles Sasseen, one of the forgotten founders of Mother's Day. Henderson's walking map, a lively document hinting at old scandals and mentioning a house used in a Madonna movie, identifies other attractive and interesting old houses in the historic area. Central Park is a good rest stop; "the oldest municipal park west of the Alleghenies," where Union troops camped during the Civil War.

Take US 60 south from Henderson to Paducah. The road runs through rich farmland: cornfields, grazing cows and sheep, massive old barns, a sign advertising "Antiques/Mulch For Sale," a white farmhouse surrounded by red gladioli looking like a flaming picket fence. Mattoon is the center of a thriving Amish community; a country store, roadside stands, and hand-lettered signs in farmhouse yards offer produce, crafts, and furniture for sale.

Marion, the county seat of Crittenden County, is near one of the last car ferries crossing the Ohio River to Cave-in-Rock, Illinois. (Take KY 91 north to the river.) Another distinction: Marion's jail is among the top ten jails in the country, according to a survey in *Playboy* magazine. Inmates like being able to order out for pizza. We stopped in Marion for a picnic lunch and found a large park on the outskirts of town with three tennis courts, two softball diamonds, two basketball courts, a volleyball court, a playground, and picnic tables, in a pleasant setting . . . and no one in sight on a sunny Saturday afternoon. (Driving through town on US 60, watch for park signs.)

US 60 crosses the Cumberland River at Smithland and then the Tennessee River, just before Paducah. Once the wildest of the river towns, Paducah is now happy to be known as

Quilting, a traditional Appalachian craft, becomes an art

"Quilt City USA." Every spring when Derby crowds are roaring into Louisville, a sedate gathering of 30,000 or so arrives in Paducah for the annual four-day Quilt Festival.

If that doesn't sound exciting, you haven't seen the Museum of the American Quilter's Society, or MAQS, near Paducah's waterfront. It's a new museum, opened in 1991, cool and contemporary in style. A plaque over the entrance announces its purpose: "Honoring Today's Quilter." More than 200 quilts are on display, old and new, in amazing variety. Traditional quilts. Abstract quilts. Homey quilts. Humorous quilts. Beautiful quilts. Quiet quilts. Quilts that shimmer.

Quilts that seem to explode. It doesn't take long to see quilts in a new light. This is art.

As in any museum, you hear some interesting comments. Someone was insisting, to an incredulous friend, that Dwight Eisenhower was a secret quilter. Someone else warned against using polished cotton: "It comes in beautiful colors, but it's terrible to sew on." Two women stood together, studying an intricate quilt. First woman: "How long do you think it would take to make a quilt like that?" Second woman, after a pause: "I don't know. I only know *I* wouldn't live long enough."

The Quilt Festival coincides with Paducah's Dogwood Festival—another reason why hotels, motels, and restaurants are booked solid in late April, and late arrivals look for rooms all over the area.

Other points of interest: Paducah offers an art museum, the Market House theater, and the General William Clark Market House Museum, which contains a 112-year-old drugstore. (It's much more inviting than the drugstores I'm familiar with.) Paducah's waterfront is mostly floodwall, but you'll find a gap where you can see the river. You can also cruise down the Ohio on a stern-wheeler called the *Jubilee 1.*

Paducah was founded in 1827 by explorer William Clark, who'd bought that part of Kentucky—37,000 acres—for $5.00 an acre a few years earlier. According to legend, he named the town for his Chickasaw friend, Chief Paduke. A statue of Paduke, looking noble, stands at Jefferson and 19th streets. Historians, refusing to be intimidated, say that Paduke never existed. Other names associated with Paducah are Alben W. Barkley, a U.S. senator and vice-president under President Harry Truman, and the Kentucky humorist, Irvin S. Cobb. Final fact: Paducah has more historical markers than any other city in Kentucky. My kind of town!

In the Area

All telephone numbers are within area code 502.

Otter Creek Park. For information write: Park Manager, Otter Creek Park Rd., Vine Grove, KY 40175, or call 583-3577.

Fort Knox Public Affairs Office, P.O. Box 995, Fort Knox, KY 40121-5000.

Patton Museum of Cavalry and Armor. Open weekdays, 9:00 a.m.-4:30 p.m; weekends and holidays, May 1 through Sept. 30, 10:00 a.m.-6:00 p.m.; Oct. 1 through April 30, 10:00 a.m.-4:30 p.m.

The Doe Run Inn, Brandenburg, KY. 422-2042.

Brandenburg: Meade County Chamber of Commerce, 734 High St., P.O. Box 483, Brandenburg, KY 40108. 422-3426.

Hardinsburg-Cloverport: Breckinridge County Tourism, P.O. Box 554, Hardinsburg, KY 40143.

Hawesville: Hancock County Chamber of Commerce, P.O. Box 404, Hawesville, KY 42348.

John James Audubon State Park, Box 576, Henderson, KY 42420-0576. 826-2247 or 1-800-255-PARK

Thomason's Bar-B-Que, Atkinson St. 826-0654.

Marion: Crittenden Chamber of Commerce, P.O. Box 164, Fohs Hall, N. Walker St., Marion, KY 42064-0164. 965-5015 or 1-800-755-0361.

Paducah: Paducah-McCracken County Tourist and Convention Commission, P.O. Box 90, Paducah, KY 42001. 1-800-359-4775.

Museum of the American Quilters' Society, 2155 Jefferson St. 442-8856.

The Market House (including Market House Museum),
Broadway at Second St. Open Tuesday through
Saturday, noon-4:00 p.m.; Sunday, 1:00-5:00 p.m.
Closed January-February, except for weekends.

4 ~

Southwest Kentucky: "The Purchase"

Take I-24 north from Paducah to KY 358 and 473 west. The tour from Paducah including Hickman and Madrid Bend to Kenlake Park is about 218 miles. The tour from Paducah including Mayfield and Princeton to Pennyrile Park is about 173 miles.

Highlights: *Water lilies and cypress swamps, wildlife areas, Indian mounds, the Mississippi River, a Civil War battlefield, cemetery sculpture in Mayfield, Adsmore House and Pennyrile State Resort Park, the Land Between the Lakes, and memories of moonshine.*

In 1818 General Andrew Jackson and Governor Isaac Shelby bought 8,500 square miles of wilderness west of the Tennessee River from the Chickasaw Indians for $300,000—a famous real estate investment that became known as the Jackson Purchase, or, in Kentucky, simply the Purchase. It contains eight counties in western Kentucky; Paducah, Murray, and Mayfield are the largest towns.

From Paducah, take I-24 north to the Maxon exit. Follow KY 358 and 473 west to Monkey's Eyebrow. (It's a good idea to gas up in Paducah. You may not find another gas station until

Wickliffe.) Driving toward Monkey's Eyebrow, you see flat farmland, cornfields, cows and horses out grazing, black-eyed Susans and Queen Anne's lace growing beside the road, a sign proclaiming "Coon Hunters For Sale."

On a Sunday morning, the many small churches were surrounded by muddy cars and trucks. We saw more cardinals than we've ever seen before and luxuriant stands of rose of Sharon bushes. In Bandana, we stopped at a hardware store to check directions and were told to "turn right and when the road dead-ends, go left on KY 473. You have to keep an eye out for Monkey's Eyebrow—ain't much there." We asked about the name and the Bandana man sighed patiently. As usual, there are several stories to choose from. "They say, if you look at a map of this place, it looks like a monkey and up there is the eyebrow. A little moonshine might help you see it."

All we saw was a shed, a house, a parked car, and a sign: "Monkey's Eyebrow. Duck and Goose Processing." Two hunting dogs, held behind a wire fence, barked furiously as we drove by.

KY 473, turning south, leads to the village of Oscar and the Ballard County Wildlife Management Area. In July, it was hot and very quiet, with hawks circling in the sky. Entering the preserve, you first see muddy water choked with water lilies, stretching out into the distance—a scene reminiscent of the Louisiana bayous. A gravel road leads on through a meadow. We saw deer running into the woods; other visitors have seen 100 deer standing motionless in the meadow at twilight. Farther in, there's a cypress swamp where frogs splashed and croaked in the shadows, a lake, and some primitive campsites. The fishing—bass, crappie, bluegill, catfish, carp, and buffalo—is said to be very good, but the two fishermen we saw were sound asleep on a dock.

The Ballard wildlife area totals 8,373 acres, with twenty miles of gravel roads, and forms part of the Mississippi Flyway, a natural migratory path for ducks and geese flying south. A list of threatened and endangered species in the area includes, besides bald and golden eagles, some names worth knowing: the Mississippi kite, the bird-voiced treefrog, the orange-footed pimpleback, and the taillight shiner.

At KY 1105, go right to Barlow. Turn right at the church and take US 60 south to Wickliffe. Ancestors of the Chickasaw Indians, called the Mound Builders or the Mississippian people, were the first known inhabitants of Wickliffe from about 800 to 1500 A.D. The advantages of the location are still obvious: high bluffs safe from floods, rich and fertile bottom land, and a sweeping view of the Mississippi and Ohio rivers merging at a point where Kentucky, Ohio, and Missouri meet.

The Wickliffe Mounds museum has a ten-minute video presentation, a small gift shop, and a self-guided tour of five sites. The Mound Builders were farmers and traders, not warriors; no weapons, except one flint dagger, have ever been found.

The museum's highlight is its exhibit on the continuing controversy surrounding Indian mounds and the conflicting claims of archaeologists and Native Americans; the conclusion is that the problems can probably be resolved, with good will on both sides. Meanwhile, "the biggest threat to burials and other sites is growing worse—looting and land vandalism. Artifact hunters selfishly destroy thousands of sites every year." Other interests in Wickliffe are indicated by signs advertising country ham, sorghum molasses, cashews, and quail. There's a bridge across the Ohio to Cairo, Illinois.

Take US 51/62 south to Bardwell. Take KY 123 south to Columbus and the Columbus-Belmont Battlefield State Park. *Note:* US 51/62, called "the Great River Road," is a scenic route passing through four Kentucky counties. The road has much to recommend it, but it's not very near the river.

Columbus is a quiet village with a name that recalls grandiose old ideas. After the Louisiana Purchase in 1803 and the burning of Washington, D.C., in the War of 1812, land speculators tried to sell this place as the natural geographic center of the country, a much safer spot than Washington and, they hoped, the next capital of the United States. Engineers drew up ambitious plans for a city named Columbus; the plans still exist in the records of the county courthouse. And the name remains.

The Civil War brought more grandiose ideas; Columbus would be the Confederacy's "Gibraltar of the West." Nineteen thousand Confederate troops under General Leonidas Polk were stationed here, 140 heavy guns were mounted on the bluffs, and a huge chain was stretched across the river to the Missouri side. (It soon broke.) A second Confederate camp was set up across the river at Belmont, Missouri.

In the fall of 1861, General U. S. Grant occupied Paducah and Cairo; that November, he attacked the Confederate fort at Belmont. The attack was successful; a later attack on Columbus failed. "We must cut our way out as we cut our way in," General Grant ordered. More than 1,000 men died. You can still see a network of earthen trenches in the park, as well as the great anchor, a few remaining links of the river chain, and the barrel of a massive Confederate cannon. A frame building, once a Confederate field hospital, is now a small museum. The exhibits vary; a couple of department store mannequins have been dressed in Union and Confederate uniforms, but in spite of the boots, spurs, swords, and campaign hats, they retain a distinctly feminine air.

The park, open from April through October, has magnificent views of the Mississippi, hiking trails, campsites, and a playground. A father overheard speaking to two children climbing on the cannon: "First we'll go to the museum. *Then* we'll get ice cream and play miniature golf."

You have two choices on leaving the Columbus-Belmont Battlefield Park. The first route goes south to Hickman, the second east to Mayfield. Both conclude at the Land Between the Lakes.

Columbus to Hickman

Take KY 123 south to Cayce. Take KY 94 west to Hickman. In the summer, this is lush, tropical-looking land. The road crosses the Bayou du Chien and goes by Cayce, home of the legendary railroad man Casey Jones. (There are remains of ancient Indian mounds, camps, and burial fields all along the Bayou du Chien.) The lowest point in Kentucky, 257 feet, is here in Fulton County, along the Mississippi River.

Hickman has a dramatic setting both below and on top of bluffs along the Mississippi River. The old business district is below the bluffs; the newly restored Victorian courthouse looks down from above. Many fine old houses remain from times more prosperous than the present. This is the only still-water harbor on the Mississippi between St. Louis and Memphis; thousands of tons of agricultural products are shipped out each year. Unfortunately, the town has lost its 141-year-old ferry, which closed down in 1991. Now the only way to cross the river is to drive north to Cairo, Illinois, or south to Dyersburg, Tennessee; both are fifty miles away.

In *Life on the Mississippi*, Mark Twain described Hickman as "a pretty town perched on a handsome hill." It's perched on something else as well: the New Madrid fault, which caused the country's greatest earthquakes in 1811 and 1812, felt as far north as Hartford, Connecticut.

Around here, Madrid is pronounced MAD-rid. From Hickman, you can take a look at a part of the state many Kentuckians have never heard of, although Mark Twain knew about it: New Madrid Bend, a small section of Fulton County cut off by a loop in the Mississippi River. This may have been caused by the 1812 earthquake, when, it's said, the earth heaved and the waters of the Mississippi ran backward toward their source.

Take KY 94 west to Sassafras Ridge, then south to Tiptonville, Tennessee. Take KY 22 north to Madrid Bend, Kentucky. This rich alluvial land is mostly planted in soybeans and corn. The French once called the place Greasy Bend. Farmers who live here call it "the Bend." (The rest of Kentucky is "the mainland.") They pay taxes in Kentucky but send their children to Tennessee schools. It's a curiosity. But like Monkey's Eyebrow, "Ain't much there."

After returning to Hickman, take KY 94 east to Murray. This quiet town—and the Kentucky Lake area—attracted a lot of attention when it was named the no. 1 retirement area in a survey by Rand McNally. Taxes and housing costs are low. There are good medical facilities, a low crime rate, and "unlimited outdoor recreation" (that's where Kentucky Lake comes in). Other assets are Murray State University and the National Scouting Museum.

If you're interested in antiques, take a quick side trip to Hazel, twelve miles south of Murray on US 641. It's a little town "about the size of Mayberry on the Andy Griffith show," an enthusiastic young woman said, arranging a table of "collectibles" in a Main Street shop. "Hazel was just dyin' out, like little towns do," she continued. "Then one man opened an antique store and he did well and, next thing you know, there's the Hazel Antique Mall. Thirteen shops! And more people around than you can shake a stick at. People stopping on their way up from Florida, or coming down from as far north as Washington, D.C." Hazel celebrates all this on Hazel Day, the first Saturday in October. "We have a band

and buggy rides and a cake walk and everything you could want to eat and drink. You all come down to see us, hear?"

Leaving Hazel, take US 641 north to Murray, then swing east on KY 94 to Kenlake State Resort Park, on Kentucky Lake. The park has a lodge, cottages, campsites, a marina, outdoor and indoor tennis, a pool, and golf. It's a good base for exploring the Land Between the Lakes.

Columbus to Mayfield

Leaving Columbus-Belmont Battlefield State Park, take KY 80 east to Mayfield. The scene: gently rolling country, good farmland, woods of hickory, sycamore, and oak, and more "Congested Area" signs with nobody in sight. Just past Milburn, we saw a bobcat streak across the road. Fancy Farm, ten miles west of Mayfield, is the site of the largest one-day picnic in the world, according to the *Guinness Book of World Records*, a tradition that began in 1881 and is still going strong. The picnic takes place on the first Saturday in August, with plenty of food, games, and political speeches (if you consider that an attraction).

Mayfield has the distinction of being named for a victim— an early settler who was robbed, murdered, and dumped into what is now Mayfield Creek. The Purchase District Fair and harness racing come to Mayfield in June; the World Coon Hunter Championship is held during the last week in October.

The town's most interesting asset is the Wooldridge Monuments—the grave of Henry C. Wooldridge in Maplewood Cemetery at the north end of town, on US 45. Wooldridge was by all accounts a "different" kind of man, a horse breeder and trader who planned the monument before his death in 1899. It's quite a sight: eerie, thought-provoking. And crazy. You see a standing marble figure of Wooldridge on a pedestal, another of Wooldridge mounted on his favorite horse, the vault where he lies buried; all this is surrounded by marble statues of his mother, four brothers, three sisters, two great-nieces, two favorite dogs, a fox, and a deer, who leads the parade.

The life-size figures all face east. Wooldridge, mounted on his horse, looks Napoleonic. The attending statues look solemn, resigned to their fate. It takes one side of the two-sided historical marker just to identify the cast of characters by name. The other side reads, "This rare statuary, a memorial to loved ones, was conceived by Colonel Henry Wooldridge, whose central marble image was carved in Italy. Devoted to the memory of his family and his life. Animal lover, famous fox hunter, and member of the Masonic Order. Only he is entombed here. Details at Chamber of Commerce." A woman in a red dress, with matching hat and shoes, walked all around the monument in silence. Then she said, speaking to no one in particular, "That was surely a beautiful horse. But wasn't *he* the least little man!"

On the outskirts of town, we stopped at a flea market and the proprietor asked where we were from. Michigan, we said. "I'm heading up there tomorrow," he said. "Taking sixty watermelons; that'll pay for the gas."

From Mayfield, take the Purchase Parkway northeast to Kentucky Dam Village State Resort Park, a distance of about twenty-five miles. This park is a large complex with two lodges, one overlooking Kentucky Lake, the other adjacent to an eighteen-hole golf course; seventy-two year-round cottages, various campsites also open year-round, a marina, rental fishing boats and houseboats, a pool, golf, tennis, and horseback riding, as well as a convention center and an airstrip.

Like Kenlake, Kentucky Dam Village makes a good base for exploring the many possibilities of the Land Between the Lakes. A third option is Pennyrile State Forest Resort Park, in

Dawson Springs. It is not quite as convenient—about twenty-eight miles from Eddyville on the Western Kentucky Parkway—but it is smaller and quieter, in a lovely setting in the Pennyrile State Forest. Another advantage of Pennyrile is its proximity to Adsmore House in Princeton, a historic house museum that Land Between the Lakes visitors should make an effort to see.

From Kentucky Dam Village, take the Purchase Parkway north to the Western Kentucky Parkway and go east ten miles to Princeton. Although Princeton has many handsome old houses, the town is dominated, as the owners probably intended, by Adsmore, a large Greek Revival house, built in 1857, that nearly overflows its in-town lot. Adsmore, described as "Kentucky's only living house museum," tells the history of a Victorian family, and their era, through their possessions. The family, founded by a penniless young man who fled the potato famine in Ireland, became within a few generations the model of rich, well-connected, small-town aristocracy.

Adsmore illustrates the eloquence of things, from a Victorian pier glass mirror, to lace curtains, to a pair of kid gloves left on an end table. Everything is original: the wallpaper, the furniture, the china, the silver, the dresses and hats, the books, the collection of clocks. (The family's clothes were preserved for years in steamer trunks with crumbled tobacco leaves between the folds.) Adsmore's guided tours have themes that vary with the seasons. We were there for a summer wedding (Selena Smith marrying Governor John Osborne in 1907); there's a Valentine's Day party, Easter, Selena's springtime engagement party, a fall harvest celebration, Christmas, and a Victorian wake in January.

"Return with me to the year 1907," began the costumed guide as she combined a description of wedding customs with Garrett family history. She explained that an unmarried girl would put a slice of the groom's cake under her pillow to bring

Adsmore where you can "return to the year 1907 "

dreams of the man she would marry, and quoted a disap-
pointed lady as saying, "But all I ever got was a stiff neck and
a pile of crumbs." It's an artful and effective presentation. Our
group responded enthusiastically. "I can't believe how interesting it was, all that old stuff," a young man wearing a "Hot
Tubbing in Dallas" T-shirt said to his girlfriend on the way out.

If you're staying at Pennyrile Forest State Resort Park, from Princeton, take KY 62 east to Dawson Springs. Follow the signs south to Pennyrile Forest State Resort Park. Or return to the Western Kentucky Parkway and go east to Dawson Springs. Dawson Springs was once a resort town, known for its mineral water and health spas, and it still retains a welcoming, resortlike air. The Pennyrile Forest State Resort Park is named for a tiny wild mint plant, also known as the pennyroyal, which gives its name to a large region of Kentucky. (Once abundant, the plant is now very hard to find.) Surrounded by 15,000 acres of forest, Pennyrile Park offers a lake, eight miles of hiking and nature trails, tennis, golf, a lodge, cottages, and campsites.

It's interesting to know, when you're out on the trails, that the area's first settler, John Thompson, arrived in 1808 with his wife, young son, and a yoke of oxen after a perilous journey through the Cumberland Gap and down Daniel Boone's Wilderness Road. The family spent the first year under a rock shelter, living on wild game. "Today this site is surrounded by the hiking trails, playgrounds, and swimming area of Pennyrile Forest State Resort Park," says a park brochure.

The Jacob Morriss family arrived in 1810, and "their graves are found on the golf course in the shade of a sycamore on a hill overlooking Clifty Creek." Our cottage at Pennyrile was quiet and comfortable, with a screened porch so sheltered by trees it felt like a tree house. "Nice around here, isn't it?" a man in the next cottage said when we met on the road. "But noisy. All those fireflies and songbirds. . . ."

To return to the Land Between the Lakes, take the Western Kentucky Parkway west to Eddyville. The Land Between the Lakes (LBL) was once the land between the Tennessee and Cumberland rivers—an isolated and sparsely populated area of farms, iron furnaces, and moonshine stills. During the

Prohibition years, from 1920 until 1933, the tiny town of Golden Pond was widely known as the "moonshine capital of the world."

According to Joe Creason's Kentucky book: "Three ferries were the only means of crossing the rivers in those days and sentries on horseback were posted at the landings to spread the alarm. . . . If anyone faintly resembling an agent was spotted, the sentries would ride to the nearest farmhouse and start ringing the dinner bell. The alarm would be picked up and passed along until the area echoed to the slow, metallic clang of dinner bells. . . . Still fires would be extinguished, barrels hidden, and bottled stock concealed. Once the danger was past, the all-clear was sounded by three blasts from a shotgun."

Al Capone's mob relied so heavily on Golden whiskey that there were rumors of a landing strip and planes from Chicago making regular stops. After repeal, the area was still known for its moonshine. A popular politician used to tell the voters, "I'm for you 110 proof, and that's as high as I can make it!" But in 1944 everything began to change. The Tennessee Valley Authority dammed the Tennessee River, creating Kentucky Lake and bringing electrical power to the region. In 1961 the TVA proposed damming the Cumberland River and creating a "national recreation area." Bitter opposition arose from most of the local people, but their efforts failed. The project was approved by President Kennedy and funded and signed into law by President Johnson in 1964.

Almost 900 families were moved from their homes in Kentucky and Tennessee; the Kentucky towns of Fenton, Golden Pond, Hematite, and Energy disappeared. The next year, waters from the Cumberland River poured into Lake Barkley, creating the Land Between the Lakes.

The two lakes make up the largest man-made body of water in the world, with a combined 3,600 miles of shoreline and 220,000 surface acres of water; a playground for sailors, houseboaters, water sports enthusiasts, and people who like to fish. Houseboats are very popular; some people live on them year-round. More usually, a family will rent a houseboat and cruise the lake waters for a week or so, enjoying a "summertime and the livin' is easy" vacation. One report: "They say you can operate a houseboat if you can drive a car, and I guess that's true. We had a wonderful time. But we did knock down a dock or two, coming in to shore."

A frequent LBL visitor suggests that when you're back in your car, you should "follow KY 453 to Grand Rivers for lunch or dinner at Patti's 1880 restaurant. Try the Kentucky Hot Brown, the pork chops, or the sawdust pie."

The TVA has ambitious plans for this area, seeing it as "a national demonstration in outdoor recreation, environmental education, and resource management." The LBL Golden

A tobacco barn

Pond Visitor Center features a planetarium and an exhibit on the moonshine era. Homeplace 1850, a "living history farm," is made up of barns and log buildings moved from their original sites: a cabin, dogtrot house, tobacco barn, springhouse, etc. Attendants in period dress illustrate the work of an 1850 farm family with the help of a yoke of oxen. (Interesting if you're a city type who's been wondering what a yoke of oxen is.) The Woodlands Nature Center has a pair of red wolves, bald and golden eagles, deer, coyotes, and owls, as well as snakes, fish and turtles, a black vulture, and a red-tailed hawk. Something for everyone!

The Trace, a forty-mile road, runs down the peninsula between the lakes into Tennessee. Watch for deer, wild turkeys, and, in the summer, wild raspberries growing along the road.

In the Area

All numbers are within area code 502.

Ballard Wildlife Management Area, RR 1, La Center, KY 42056. 224-2244. Closed October 15–March 14.

Wickliffe Mounds Museum & Archaeological Site, P.O. Box 155, Wickliffe, KY 42087. 335-3681.

Columbus-Belmont State Park, P.O. Box 8, Columbus, KY 42032-0008. 677-2327.

Hickman Chamber of Commerce, 109A Clinton St., Hickman, KY 42058. 236-2902.

Murray Tourism Commission, 805 N. 12th St., P.O. Box 190, Dept. KTG, Murray, KY 42071. 753-5171.

Kenlake State Resort Park, Route 1, Box 522, Hardin, KY 42048-9737. 1-800-325-0143.

Mayfield-Graves County Tourist Commission, P.O. Box 468, Mayfield, KY 42066. 247-6101.

Kentucky Dam Village State Resort Park, P.O. Box 69, Gilbertsville, KY 42044-0069. 1-800-325-1046.

Adsmore Museum, 304 N. Jefferson St., Princeton, KY 42445. 365-3114. Open Tuesday through Saturday, 11:00 a.m.-4:00 p.m.; Sunday, 1:30-4:00 p.m.

Pennyrile Forest State Resort Park, 20781 Pennyrile Lodge Rd., Dawson Springs, KY 42408-9212. 1-800-325-1711.

Patti's Restaurant, 100 Main St., Grand Rivers, KY 42045. 362-8844.

Land Between the Lakes, 100 Van Morgan Drive, Golden Pond, KY 42211-9001. 924-5602.

5 ~

North-Central Kentucky to the Eastern Mountains

Take I-75 south from Cincinnati to I-275 west. Pick up 546 south to KY 8.

Highlights: *Augusta and Maysville, two historic river towns; a ferry, covered bridges, and log cabins in the village of Washington; two state resort parks; W-Hollow, home of mountain poet and novelist Jesse Stuart; a coal baron's mansion in Ashland; folk art and chocolate sodas in Morehead, and an Antique Weapons Hunting Area.*

Kentucky is defined by its rivers, which mark the state borders in three directions: to the east, the Big Sandy and the Tug Fork; to the north, the Ohio; to the west, the Mississippi River. Altogether, Kentucky has about 3,000 miles of navigable river—more than any other state. It's not always possible to follow the rivers through Kentucky; floods have forced roads back to a prudent distance in many areas. But a major river is always a powerful presence, in or out of sight.

On I-75, driving south from Cincinnati, cross the river and take I-275 east to Wilder. Follow the "AA" highway, 546,

Cross the Ohio on the Augusta ferry

south to Foster; turn left and go one-quarter mile to KY 8; turn right toward Augusta. From Augusta on the Ohio River to Ashland in the Eastern Highlands and back to Maysville by way of Morehead and the Daniel Boone National Forest is a distance of about 280 miles.

Augusta is only thirty-five miles from Cincinnati, but it feels much farther; you are, it seems, suddenly in the rural South. Driving east on KY 8, you see burley tobacco leaves drying in small barns, trees overhanging the road, railroad tracks, and the wide blue waters of the Ohio on the left. Just past a sign that reads "Mowing Zone," Augusta comes into view. An old hillside cemetery, where stone angels and cherubs stand guard by sinking tombstones, overlooks the town below. A mossy inscription reads: "Under this mound the form of a loved one, whose memory our thoughts and affections still dwell on . . ."

Augusta, founded in 1798, was built on the site of an ancient Indian burial ground. The town was once a bustling river port, the site of "the first Methodist college in the world" (small towns love world-wide claims), vineyards, and a winery. Only the winery remains—a massive limestone structure off KY 8 at the east end of town.

Defying the danger of floods, Augusta's riverfront is open and inviting. You see fishermen on the river banks, barges and pleasure boats going by, a ferry approaching its dock with flag flying. Boat whistles blow and people wave back at the pilots.

The ferry, which began in 1798 with John Boude's ferry service, crosses the river between Augusta and Boude's Landing in Ohio most of the year, with crossings often "by request." It's very much a part of the local scene; parties have begun on the ferry and moved on to dinner at the Beehive Tavern.

Buildings from the pioneer, Federal, and Victorian periods line Riverside Drive, enhanced by brick walks, boxwood, flowers, and patios overlooking the river. The old houses and the open river setting attract TV and movie directors. Parts of *Centennial* and *Huckleberry Finn* were filmed here. Most recently a Neil Simon movie, *Lost in Yonkers*, was shot here, with the Ohio standing in for the Hudson River.

Augusta's walking tour map, a detailed document, lists fifty-four buildings, including a waterfront house owned by singer Rosemary Clooney and an 1861 house "said to have had the first bathroom in Augusta." The Piedmont Gallery, in a 1795 riverfront building, has a fine collection of contemporary and antique arts and crafts. Nearby, the Beehive Tavern occupies a corner building that was a drugstore when it was hit by Morgan's Raiders in 1862. The Lamplighter Inn on Second Street serves dinner on Friday and Saturday nights and a brunch on Sunday; weekend "mysteries," with the guests playing sleuth, are a Lamplighter specialty.

Augusta holds an Arts and Crafts Festival and Stern-wheeler Regatta on the third weekend in June, and a street fair with historic home tours on the Labor Day weekend. Augusta is in Bracken County, Maysville in Mason County. Germantown is between the two, right on the county line. The "Old Reliable" Germantown Fair and Horse Show, begun in 1854 and one of the oldest in the state, is held during the first week in August.

Head east on KY 8 to Maysville. Leaving Augusta, look for the limestone winery on the left, its large stone cellar built into the side of a hill. Many of Augusta's early settlers were German immigrants from the Rhine Valley, who must have been reminded of home when they planted grapevines on slopes near the Ohio. The product was Baker wine, a light rosé that sold well until 1850, when a tornado ripped through the vineyards. Blight finished off what was left in the next few years. The vineyards were turned into peach orchards, and tobacco became the important money crop.

Founded in 1783, Maysville was first called Limestone Landing, because that's what it was: a likely spot for settlers coming down the Ohio on flatboats to disembark. The early settlers didn't linger long, due to the threat of Shawnee Indians just across the river, but made their way up the hill to a cluster of cabins that became a town called Washington.

Maysville is immediately appealing—a town clinging to a steep hillside of terraces that descend to the river. The hilltop view is dramatic: rooftops, green trees, the white spire of the Mason County courthouse, and the spans of the Simon Kenton Bridge crossing the river to Aberdeen, Ohio.

The historic district is eight blocks long and three blocks wide, an easy and rewarding walk. Many of the buildings date from the early 1800s and the steamboat era, when merchants took the farmers' tobacco, whiskey, and cattle down the river on consignment, sold them where they would bring

The steeples of Maysville

the best price, and came back with household goods and luxuries from New Orleans. The legacy of those days is evident in ornate iron grillwork on many houses; others show exuberant touches of Steamboat Gothic trim. Ask someone at the Maysville-Mason County Tourism Commission about another unusual architectural detail—the "descending parapets." The Commission offers guided walking and bus tours of Maysville and Washington as well as walking tour maps.

The Mason County Museum, on Sutton Street, has exhibits and documents of the area's pioneer days—a savage history with memorable characters like Daniel Boone, his friend and fellow scout Simon Kenton, and a fierce Shawnee chief named Blue Jacket. They all appear in *The Frontiersman,* an exciting novel by Allan Eckert. A Likely Story, a bookstore on Second Street, has copies.

Maysville is rediscovering its waterfront. "We have a hole in our wall now, just like Paducah!" a Maysville resident remarked with pride. This means an opening in the floodwall, a riverside park, and a boulder possibly initialed by Daniel Boone. Daniel Boone and his wife operated a tavern in Maysville for a few years. Later taverns displayed signs saying, "Bed, Board & Bourbon, 2 Bits." Today's visitors should try Caproni's, on Rosemary Clooney Street, for a good meal and a river view. (Don't worry when the train roars by your window; it hasn't hit the restaurant yet.) Conversation overheard at Caproni's: "Why are the tobacco barns always painted black?" "Because tar is cheaper than paint."

Maysville is home to eighteen tobacco warehouses, conducts tobacco auctions from late November through mid-January, and claims to be the "second largest burley tobacco market in the world"—a claim also made by Carrollton. And the largest burley tobacco market in the world? That's Lexington, Kentucky.

Go east on Third Street, past the historic district and the bridge, and turn right on US 68. This leads up and over the hill to Washington, three miles south. Although now incorporated into Maysville, Washington is a distinct village, a pioneer town founded in 1785 on land bought from Simon Kenton for 50 cents an acre. Only Harrodsburg is older.

The town had its days of glory. In 1792, when Kentucky became a state, Washington was the second largest town and the county seat, with a population of 462; it had 119 log houses, the state's first public water system (twenty-two wells), schools, shops, churches, three rope walks, and, in 1798, the first post office west of the Alleghenies. No wonder the town was known as a "center of fashion and education." But once the Indian raids stopped and river traffic increased, Maysville began to grow and Washington began to fade. In 1848, Maysville became the county seat. As the years went by, Washington nearly disappeared.

Historic preservation saved Washington and its pioneer buildings in the 1970s. Now guides in costume lead tours to the 1819 Paxton Inn, the 1803 Albert Sidney Johnson birthplace (Johnson was a Confederate general, killed at the battle of Shiloh), the Old Church Museum, the Simon Kenton Historic Site, and the 1787 Mefford's Station, a house "built of boards from the flatboat on which George Mefford, his wife, and thirteen children descended the Ohio."

Houses built by Arthur Fox and William Wood, who bought the land from Simon Kenton, still stand. Behind the 1800 Marshall Key house is a small brick smokehouse with gunslits, used as a refuge during Indian attacks. Federal Hill, a brick Colonial house, overlooks Washington; it was built in 1798 by Thomas Marshall, whose brother was the first chief justice of the United States. Their mother's grave is in the family graveyard, its inscription faint but still striking: "Mary Randolph Keith . . . she was good, not brilliant, useful, not ornamental, and the mother of 13 children."

Washington celebrates with a number of festivals. The most colorful is its Frontier Christmas on the first weekend of December, when pioneer scouts, British officers, and Shawnees appear, carolers in costume burst into song, bell-ringers play carols, and a horse pulling a surrey clops down the street. Several special events are part of Frontier Christmas; last year's winner was an enchanting "Celebration of Fashion," with members of the Maysville Players modeling clothes from 1792 to 1940. (Most of the outfits came from Maysville and Washington attics.)

In spite of an abundance of antique shops, Washington has its own honest, homespun charm. When the streets are nearly empty, the shops are closed, and the air is blue with twilight mist and faintly scented with wood smoke, the pioneer past can be strongly felt, like a ghost.

Take US 68 back to Maysville, KY 10 east to Tollesboro, KY 57 north to Concord, and KY 8 to Vanceburg. KY 10 is also known as the Mary Ingles Trail, in memory of the legendary Mary Ingles, who was captured by a war party of Mingo Indians in 1766. After surviving terrible hardships, she escaped near Big Bone Lick and made her way back to her home in the mountains. Route 10 follows her escape route.

"That's a lonesome road," a Maysville friend said of KY 8, and he was right; lonesome, lovely, and restful. We seldom saw another car as we headed toward Vanceburg and the mountains; we drove up and down hills and valleys, past a few farms, and through woods showing the first bright signs of fall. We had no way of testing our friend's firm belief that people in Lewis County, to the east of Maysville, are noticeably different from folks in Mason County. And as for people across the river in Ohio . . . well! "It's a surprise," he said, "that we even speak the same language."

Mason County has two covered bridges. The Valley Pike Bridge is the only privately owned covered bridge in Kentucky (off old highway 10 on Valley Pike Road). Dover Bridge is on KY 1235 (Tuckahoe Road) near the junction with KY 8 at Dover. Lewis County has one: the Cabin Creek Bridge on KY 984, 4.5 miles northwest of Tollesboro, and near what was once an Indian war road.

We met travelers who were happily spending a "covered bridges weekend" in northern Kentucky and knew all about the difference between the "burr truss design," "yellow pine trusses," the "unusual Queensport truss," and so on. Then there are those who specialize in stone fences. Or tobacco barns. Whatever floats your boat, as the saying goes.

Vanceburg, a small town nearly surrounded by steep hills, is the county seat of Lewis County. Before the courthouse stands the only monument to Union soldiers south of the Mason-Dixon line.

Having reserved a cottage at Carter Caves State Resort Park, we stopped at a store for groceries. It's curious that shopping, a chore at home, can be such a pleasure when traveling. At the Vanceburg store, two teenage clerks were arranging milk cartons in the dairy section. Actually one was doing the work and the other was demonstrating dance steps. I asked if they had any 1/2 percent milk. "No, ma'am, we surely don't," said the dancer, doing a pretty good pirouette.

Take KY 59 south from Vanceburg to I-64. Go west on I-64 to Olive Hill and follow the signs to Carter Caves Park. KY 59 goes past tiny towns with names like Kinniconick and Head of Grassy, moving closer to the mountains. We saw a sign saying "30.06 Riffle for Sale," and another, my favorite: "New and Used Antiques."

Carter Caves State Resort Park, thirty miles west of Ashland, has 1,000 acres of forests, hills, natural rock bridges, caves, and mountain streams. The lodge overlooks Smoky Valley Lake. There are cottages and campsites, guided cave tours and canoe trips down Tygart's Creek, hiking trails, tennis, golf, and a pool. And the first voice we heard, coming into the lodge to register, was a child wailing, "Mom, there's nothing to do!" The park has twenty explored caves, three of them lighted for tours: Cascade Cave, which has an underground river and a waterfall, X Cave, and Saltpetre Cave. Bat Cave in winter is home to the endangered Indiana bat, so tours of this cave are offered only in the summer months. The social bat, on the U.S. list of vanishing species, also calls Bat Cave home. (A *social* bat? Not if I see it first.)

If you'd like to try spelunking, come to the Carter Caves Crawlathon, the first weekend in February, when instruction and special tours are offered.

In mid-September, the night was cold, the morning sunny and warm. We passed up a cave tour for a hike on Cascade Trail, near Cascade Cave. "It is perhaps our most scenic trail and passes some of the most unusual geologic features in the park, including the Cascade natural bridge, the Box Canyon, and the Wind Tunnel," says a park brochure. *Note:* Cascade Cave is not within the park grounds. Take KY 182 south, turn west on KY 209, and follow signs. The Northeastern Kentucky History Museum, open from March through October, is on KY 182.

On the trail, we found the Wind Tunnel silent, due to lack of wind, but everything else was as promised . . . wonderful. The trail goes up and down, through trees and ferns, over and around boulders and exposed tree roots, and through a narrow opening between great rocks near the Natural Bridge. One moment you're surrounded by the squarish boulders of Box Canyon; a few minutes later you see nothing but trees and sunlight and the mountains beyond.

Greenbo Lake State Park is not far from Carter Caves. Take I-64 east to Grayson and follow the park signs. We took KY 2, a more leisurely route. More black barns and bundles of golden tobacco leaves, cut and tied. Steep hills, rusty trailers, and battered houses clustered together in the hollows. A towerlike iron furnace crumbled around a tree that had grown through its chimney. At one point, we were stopped by road construction and a young woman holding up a "Stop" sign. She was wearing a black jersey, trim white pants, and hiking boots and looked like a *Vogue* model. Smoking furiously and speaking in a strong country-mountain accent, she continued a good-natured argument with another worker. "Okay, do that and he gonna whup the hound out of you," she said, laughing. Then she reversed the sign to "Go" and waved us on.

The clifftop lodge at Greenbo Lake State Park is named for Jesse Stuart, who was born in a one-room cabin a few miles away. His father, a tenant farmer, "had never gone to school a day in his life," Stuart wrote, and was illiterate. His mother "could read a book slowly and write a letter. She had completed the second grade." Jesse Stuart's writing was devoted to the Appalachian countryside and the hard, isolated life of the people who lived there. He wrote, he said, "about birds, cornfields, trees, wildflowers, log shacks, my own people, valleys and rivers and mists in the valleys."

The Jesse Stuart Library and Reading Room in the lodge has shelves of books and interesting items displayed under glass: a page of manuscript with pencil corrections, a few letters, Stuart's Smith Corona typewriter, an axe handle ("used making cross ties he then sold to buy his high school graduation suit"), and a hand towel his mother made from a cement sack. ("It hung from the back porch for the men to use when they came for dinner from the work field.") An annual Jesse Stuart weekend, at the end of September, features lectures, films, special exhibits, and a guided tour of W-Hollow, Jesse Stuart's home. "I used to buy tobacco from Jesse Stuart," our Maysville friend had said. "Nice man. Talked a lot."

Greenbo is a combination word, made from Boyd County and Greenup, its largest town. Greenbo Lake, long and narrow, curves around the lodge; both are surrounded by mountain forests. The park has a marina, rental boats, good fishing (black bass, bluegill, and catfish), campsites, a pool, and tennis courts. Deer and mallard ducks are everywhere. As we left the lodge, a doe and two fawns leapt across the road in a few bounds, as graceful as ballerinas. Near the park entrance stands the Buffalo Furnace, a larger, well-preserved version of the furnace-with-tree we'd seen earlier, and a reminder of the area's large pig iron production in the 1800s. On the other side of the road, a long line of mallard ducks seemed to be having a parade in a sunny meadow near the lake.

Leaving the park, turn left on KY 1 and go five miles until you see a church on the left. Turn left on the road beside the church to W-Hollow. A marker stands at the turn off KY 1: "Jesse Stuart, 1906–1984. This Kentucky poet laureate was born and lived most of his life in W-Hollow, near Greenup. An educator and prolific writer, Stuart was the author of books, short stories and poems which portray Appalachian Kentucky. His works include *The Thread That Runs So True* and *Man with a Bull-Tongue Plow.*"

A narrow road runs through W-Hollow, now the Jesse Stuart State Nature Preserve, bordered in places by split-rail fences, daisies, and goldenrod. A compound of one large log house, surrounded by two smaller houses, is on the left. The large house was Jesse Stuart's home and is private property. Otherwise, visitors are welcome in W-Hollow. Readers of Stuart's books will feel right at home.

Note: Two more covered bridges are near here. The Oldtown bridge is nine miles south, off KY 1, and the 1855 Bennett's Mill bridge is north on KY 7.

Leaving W-Hollow, take KY 2 to Greenup, then head east on US 23 to Ashland. Greenup is thought to be the site of Kentucky's first settlement, built by Shawnee Indians and French fur traders before 1753, and also the point from which Daniel Boone left Kentucky. (Sometime around 1799, Boone took a canoe up the Ohio to West Virginia.) Situated at the confluence of the Ohio and the Big Sandy rivers, Greenup was isolated and nearly destroyed by the 1937 floods.

It makes a difference, seeing Greenup, to know that Jesse Stuart, at age fourteen, walked five miles to and from town every day to work with a crew paving Greenup's streets. He carried 100-pound bags of cement to the concrete mixer and was paid $3.00 a day. "The same streets have withstood the years, with minor repairs," he wrote in 1974, "and are a monument to me."

Northeast Kentucky has abundant natural resources: coal, iron ore, fire clay, sandstone, limestone, oil, and gas. Driving from Greenup, you'll notice how quickly the mountain scenery turns industrial; you see a long line of gaunt and often dramatic buildings, from rusty old mills to modern steel and oil-refining plants. Ashland Oil and Armco Steel both have their headquarters in Ashland.

Ashland, eastern Kentucky's largest city, was founded in 1786 by the Poage family from Virginia and was first known, logically enough, as Poage Settlement. (The Clinton Furnace, an iron furnace built by the Poage brothers in 1833, still stands near the intersection of US 60 and KY 538.) Fortunes made in the iron, coal, and lumber industries are reflected in the Victorian-era houses included in Ashland's two-mile Historic Walking Tour; the houses range from classic Georgian to Gothic Incredible. Most impressive is the Mayo Manor on the corner of Bath and Sixteenth streets, now the Kentucky Highlands Museum.

John Caldwell Calhoun Mayo, born in 1864 in a log cabin on a Pike County farm, lived one version of the American dream. He became a coal baron and the richest man in Kentucky before he died, at the age of forty-nine, at the Waldorf Astoria Hotel in New York City.

His career began in Paintsville, where he taught school for $40.00 a month. He put himself through college, studied geology, and quickly saw buried treasure in the mineral rights of eastern Kentucky land. Soon he was buying up options on mineral rights for 50 cents to $5.00 an acre from poor farmers. "Mr. Mayo," a historian at the museum said dryly, "was not universally beloved."

No matter. At the age of thirty-three, John Mayo married Alice Jane Meek, a twenty-year-old postal clerk in Paintsville, who worked with him. On mineral-rights buying trips, she wore a riding skirt with hidden pockets full of gold coins. After her husband's death in 1914, Alice Mayo moved to Ashland, built the baronial Mayo Manor—a three-story marble building with entrances through Renaissance porches—and gave fabulous parties. Guests from New York arrived by special train, and snow was shipped from the mountains for amusing snowball fights. It was all a very long way from Paintsville.

The purpose of the Kentucky Highlands Museum is to preserve and display the "history and heritage of the Kentucky Highlands." The varied and lively collections range from ancient Indian relics to a "Rodeo Drive version of Davy Crockett's deerskin suit," a satin outfit heavy with white beads and fringe, worn by country music star Wynonna Judd, a native of Ashland.

The museum has many interesting exhibits: antique wedding dresses, haunting photographs of Appalachian coal miners, a 1928 Maytag washer, a World War II War Room, and a 1955 inter-toll telephone dialing switchboard, recalling the days when a long-distance call from Kentucky to California meant hearing a series of operators, their accents changing along the way. Take the sweeping marble stairs to the third floor with its glowing stained glass ceiling and you'll find a delightful doll and doll house collection, including a tiny log cabin with an outhouse, a potato patch, and laundry on a clothesline.

The Chimney Corner Tea Room, on Carter Avenue, is handy for rest and refreshment after a museum visit. One of Ashland's oldest restaurants, it's especially popular for lunch.

Central Park, forty-seven downtown acres, has Indian mounds as well as many recreational facilities. The Ashland Area Art Gallery & Artists' Market occupies an 1892 building with a rare cast-iron front. The Paramount Arts Center is in a 1930 movie theater best described as art deco supreme. Irish Acres Antiques has twenty-six showrooms of American and European furniture, silver, china, rugs, crystal, and more. It's outside Ashland at the unlikely address of 24203 Jacks Fork, Rush, KY. (Take I-64 west to the Ashland/Cannonsburg exit and follow signs. If you miss this one, there's another Irish Acres Antiques near Lexington.)

From Ashland, take US 23 south to I-64 and go west to Morehead. Morehead, the home of Morehead State University, is a college town nestled in the northern foothills of the great Daniel Boone National Forest, which stretches south to the Tennessee border. Downtown Morehead is an attractive place, with more activity and young people around than is usual in towns of a similar size. Be sure to see the Rowan County courthouse, the university campus, and the MSU Folk Art Gallery at 119 University Avenue. Granny Toothman, a skilled spinner and weaver, is artist-in-residence at Morehead State, and some of her works—items woven from dog hair, for instance—are included in the excellent folk art collection.

The Holbrook Drugstore on Main Street, across from the courthouse, is a find for travelers who, like us, are nostalgic about real drugstores and are always looking for one. The Holbrook drugstore has the right atmosphere, friendly and soothing, and the right scent, sweet and faintly medicinal. The small soda fountain doesn't work (parts were not available to repair the spigots), but you can still sit on a stool and have a real chocolate soda, with two scoops of vanilla ice cream, for 90 cents. Or fresh lemonade (a big net bag of lemons near the cash register is reassuring). Or a piece of chocolate or vanilla fudge, made right there on a marble slab. "Seems like I heard someone say there are still four real drugstore soda fountains left in Kentucky," the nice woman behind the counter said. "But I forget where they are."

Carter Run Lake, near Morehead, was created by a dam built to control flooding in the lower Licking River. It's the "muskie fishing capital of the world," people say, and together with the Daniel Boone National Forest, forms a bountiful recreation area for hiking, backpacking, rock climbing, and white-water rafting. A Morehead art professor recommends the Poppin Rock area to photographers. From Morehead, take US 60 south to Clearfield and KY 519 south to the Poppin Rock Boat Ramp. Rent a boat, take your camera, and explore the submerged timber area ahead.

Notice the area names, like Tater Knob Trail, Farmers, Soldier, Moon, Relief, and Ordinary. The Zilpo Scenic Byway is a ridgetop road that passes through the forest's Pioneer Weapons Hunting Area. Here hunters armed with bows and arrows, crossbows, and flintlock rifles can play Daniel Boone and track the resident wild turkeys, squirrels, grouse, and white-tailed deer.

The 250-mile Sheltowee Trace Trail runs through the Daniel Boone Forest, from north of Moorehead to Pickett State Park in Tennessee. Sheltowee, a Shawnee word meaning "big turtle," was the name given to Daniel Boone when he was held captive by the Shawnees.

Leaving Morehead, take KY 32 west to Flemingsburg. Then take KY 11 north to Maysville. These roads, rolling through small towns, farms, and pastures, cut through

Fleming County, "the land of covered bridges." Three bridges remain; the Goddard White Bridge is the best known. You'll find it six miles east of Flemingsburg, on the right and in sight of the road. (If you get to Logan's Country Store in Goddard, you've gone too far.)

The bridge, spanning Sand Lick Creek, is still open to traffic. But it is photographers who find it a major attraction. They like to photograph the perfectly placed, small, white country church through the bridge. "The church burned down a few years ago," someone in Goddard said. "But they rebuilt it on the same spot. Just to keep the tourists happy, I guess."

At one time Kentucky had more than 400 covered bridges; the cover was to keep the bridges dry and prevent the trusses from rotting out. Many were destroyed during the Civil War.

On KY 11 toward Maysville you pass by more farms, old barns, horses out to pasture, and piles of bright orange pumpkins in the fields. "No surprises on that road," a man in a country store said, "but a whole lot of nice."

In the Area

All numbers are within area code 606.

For information, write City of Augusta, P.O. Box 85, Augusta, KY 41992.

The Piedmont Gallery, 115 W. Riverside Drive. 756-2216.

The Beehive Tavern, corner of Main St. and Riverside Drive. 756-2202.

The Lamplighter Inn, 103 W. Second St. 756-2603.

All the above have Augusta walking tour maps available for visitors.

Maysville-Mason County Tourism Commission, 216 Bridge St. 564-9411.

Mason County Museum, 215 Sutton St. 564-5865.

A Likely Story Bookstore, 15 W. Second St. 564-9370.

Caproni's Restaurant, Rosemary Clooney St. 564-4119.

Washington: Cane Brake Visitor's Center, 759-5604.

Carter Caves State Resort Park, R.R. #5, Box 1120, Olive Hill, KY 41164-9032. 286-4411 or 1-800-325-0059.

Greenbo Lake State Park, H.C. 60, Box 562, Greenup, KY 41144-9517. 473-7324 or 1-800-325-0083.

Jesse Stuart State Nature Preserve. 564-2886.

Ashland Area Convention and Visitors Bureau, 207 15th St. 329-1007. Walking tour maps available here.

Kentucky Highlands Museum, 1516 Bath Ave. 329-8888. Open Tuesday through Saturday, 10:00 a.m.-4:00 p.m.; Sunday, 1:00-4:00 p.m.

Ashland Area Art Gallery & Artists' Market, 1401 Greenup Ave. 329-1826.

Paramount Arts Center, 13th and Winchester. 324-3175.

The Chimney Corner Tea Room, 1624 Carter Ave. 324-2200.

Morehead and Rowan County Tourism Commission, P.O. Box 70, Morehead, KY 40351. 784-6221.

MSU Folk Art Gallery, 119 University Ave. 783-2760.

Holbrook Drugstore, 208 E. Main St. 784-4784.

Mayor's Office, Main Cross St., Flemingsburg, KY 41041. 845-5951.

6 ~

Driving Through the Cave Country

From I-24 at Gilbertsville, take the Trace south to Golden Pond, pick up US 68 east to Cadiz and on to Bowling Green and take I-65 northeast to Mammoth Cave and Horse Cave and north to Louisville (a total of about 220 miles).

Highlights: *The scenic Land Between the Lakes Trace drive, good farmland, a string of small, appealing towns, the Knobs, the Jefferson Davis monument, country hams, antique shops, the remains of a Shaker settlement at South Union, a Corvette Museum at Bowling Green, Mammoth Cave, summer theater at Horse Cave, the American Museum of Caves & Karstlands.*

We're back on Kentucky's historic US 68, once part of an ambitious plan for a "national road" extending from Zanesville, Ohio, to Florence, Alabama. Now we pick up US 68/ KY 80 in the western part of the state and travel east through the Pennyroyal section and the southern Knobs to Mammoth Cave and beyond. Along the way, the topography is interesting and unusual.

The Pennyroyal, in the south-central part of the state, sits on a limestone formation known as karst terrain. Water, eroding the porous rock, honeycombs the area with underground passages; the surface has sinkholes, ponds, and springs that may appear and disappear within days. Mammoth Cave is the best-known product of karst terrain.

The Knobs, a narrow, curving plain named for the distinctive shape of its eroded hills, forms a rough arc around the bluegrass country. Out-of-state visitors can make a game of this, asking themselves at odd moments, Is that a hill or a knob?

The Barrens, a thinly wooded, prairielike area, is best observed around the Barren River Lake State Resort Park, east of Bowling Green and near Glasgow. Indians burned off most of the original forests to provide grazing land for buffalo.

From Golden Pond, take US 68 northeast to Cadiz. The character of Cadiz (pronounced CAY-diz) changed drastically when it became the eastern gateway to Lake Barkley State Resort Park and Lake Barkley and thereby acquired a shoreline of bright blue water. (Lake Barkley, along with Kentucky Lake, forms one of the world's largest man-made lakes.) Lake Barkley State Resort Park, one of the state's largest, offers two lodges, cottages, camping sites, a conference center, a fitness center, a marina, fishing, hiking, backpacking, stables, a pool, golf, tennis, and an airstrip.

Situated at the eastern end of Lake Barkley's Little River Bay, Cadiz, the county seat of Trigg County, has become something of a tourist and retirement town. It has five antique malls and is known for its country hams. The county was named for Colonel Stephen Trigg, a Virginian frontier scout and Indian fighter, who was killed at the Battle of Blue Licks in 1782.

The Trigg County Ham Festival, held the second weekend in October, is ham-flavored to the bone. Events include a best-dressed pig award, a greased pig contest, music, hot-air balloon rides, the baking of the world's largest ham and biscuit, and a parade. Broadbent's Food & Gifts, five miles east of town on US 68, has Trigg County hams for sale.

Note: Antique stores and malls have become small-town institutions in recent years. *"Please* be positive—they're all that's keeping us going," a small-town enthusiast said. Visitors will quickly understand that the term "antiques" is used loosely and can mean anything from a museum-quality cherry highboy to a flea-market collection of chipped canning jars. Not to mention "collectibles" like scented candles and small souvenir plastic outhouses made in Taiwan. There can be real pleasure involved in small-town antique shopping if you are a good shopper, take a sporting approach to the hunt for the unusual or valuable find, or know what you're looking for. (In my case, red glass tumblers like those used at the family breakfast table when I was a child. No luck yet, but I haven't given up the search.)

Continue east on US 68 to Hopkinsville. Hopkinsville is Kentucky's sixth largest city, with a population of just under 30,000, the county seat of Christian County, and the traditional business and social center of the surrounding countryside.

One of Hopkinsville's many imposing old houses, on the National Register of Historic Places, is now Crockett's Restaurant, 317 East 16th Street, a good choice for lunch or dinner. (You might ask if there have been any recent sightings of the resident ghost.)

A pleasant place for a picnic lunch is the Round Table Literary Park on the campus of Hopkinsville Community College, which has a replica of King Arthur's Round Table and the Sword in the Stone. Don't miss the explanatory marker.

During the Civil War, Hopkinsville was the site of many skirmishes between Union and Confederate forces and changed hands at least six times. Then came the Night Riders War in 1907. At a time when the American Tobacco Company had an effective monopoly on tobacco buying, poor farmers, desperate over low tobacco prices, formed the Dark Tobacco District Planters' Protective Association and tried to retaliate

with a boycott. Desperation led to violence and vigilante justice. Masked men, calling themselves the Night Riders, tried
to terrorize uncooperative farmers with threats and whip-
pings. Tobacco fields were destroyed, barns were set on fire,
and a few murders were committed. On December 7, 1907,
250 Night Riders captured police stations in Hopkinsville, cut
off the town, and set three tobacco warehouses ablaze. In the
end, the farmers were worse off than before. The war was
over by 1909, and the American Tobacco Company won.

Much local history is on display at the Pennyroyal Area
Museum, 217 East Ninth Street, a handsome building that
was once a post office. Exhibits cover a wide range of subjects,
from the Civil War to a miniature circus. The museum has a
pioneer bedroom, a collection of old farm tools, a law office of
the early 1900s, a 1924 Ames automobile, and a Mogul Farm
Wagon made in Hopkinsville by a local company that lasted
from 1871 to 1925. (Advertising slogan: "Buy a Mogul and Will
It to Your Grandson.") Edgar Cayce, a native son and "world
famous clairvoyant" who died in 1945, is the subject of consid-
erable attention.

Except for someone in the back office, we were alone in
the Pennyroyal Museum on a sunny afternoon and spent a
rewarding hour or so looking around in a museum that has
the appeal of a well-arranged family attic.

Hopkinsville was an important stopping point in a tragic
event (and a dark chapter in American history): the forced
migration of the Cherokee nation from their southeastern
homeland to Oklahoma in the winter of 1838-39. More than
13,000 Cherokees were camped at Hopkinsville before beginning the long, deadly journey that became known as the Trail
of Tears. The original campsite is now a residential area
known as Cherokee Park.

A Trail of Tears Commemorative Park, on US 41 (Pem-
broke Road) on the west side of town, contains the graves of
two Cherokee chiefs, Whitepath and Fly Smith, who died

here. There are statues of the chiefs, a courtyard of flags representing the nine states involved in the forced march, a bronze plaque showing the route of the Trail, and a log cabin educational center by the Little River.

It's hard to think in terms of a Trail of Tears *festival*, but the Trail of Tears Intertribal Indian Pow Wow, with native crafts, traditional dancing, storytelling, food, and blowgun demonstrations, is seen as a showcase of Native American culture. It's held on the second weekend of September.

Ten miles east of Hopkinsville, an uninformed driver will suddenly see the Washington Monument standing alone in Kentucky farmland and think he, or she, is hallucinating. He, or she, can relax. It's the Jefferson Davis Monument, at 351 feet slightly shorter than the monument in Washington, D.C. Still, it's a startling sight and delivers a message as clear as the Rebel yell: "He's still our George Washington, you all!"

This is a State Historic Site and part of the park system, with a gift shop, picnic tables, and a playground.

Jefferson Davis was born here in a two-room log house, nine months before Abraham Lincoln was born near Hodgenville, less than 100 miles away. Another parallel: in 1861, Jefferson Davis was elected president of the Confederacy, less than a month before Abraham Lincoln was inaugurated as president of the United States. A historical marker, quoting from an address Jefferson Davis made at his last visit to his birthplace in 1886, gives visitors a rich burst of southern oratory: "Kentucky, my own, my native land, God grant that peace and plenty may ever run throughout your borders. God grant that your sons and daughters may ever rise to illustrate the fame of their dead fathers and that wherever the name of Kentucky is mentioned, every hand shall be lifted and every head bowed for all that is grand, all that is glorious, all that is virtuous, all that is honorable and manly."

A cheerful Kentucky Parks guide took a small group of visitors up in an elevator to the top of the monument, where we had a fine view of the road, a village store, several small houses, and green fields beyond. On the way up, she reeled off facts and figures: the world's tallest concrete obelisk, the fourth tallest monument in the United States, erected by the United Daughters of the Confederacy, financed by private donations, dedicated in 1929. On the way down, talk somehow turned to the famous 1811 earthquake at Madrid. "Lordy, lordy!" the guide said. "This part of Kentucky is just honeycombed with caves. Elkton is sitting on one of the biggest. That's where I live. If another quake hits, I don't know what will happen. Or where we'll be!"

Afterward, we walked across the road to a produce stand run by Amish farmers and picked up some beautiful peaches. All the produce—corn, tomatoes, green beans, spinach—was tempting. I asked if it was locally grown and a shy young helper shook his head. "Corn comes from Sharon Grove," he answered, honest to a fault, Sharon Grove being about twenty miles away.

A short distance from the Jefferson Davis Monument, on the right side of the road, you see a small group of old graves tilting toward the ground and sheltered by a grove of sycamore trees. It's a touching sight.

Elkton, eight miles east of the Jefferson Davis Monument, is a pleasant little town in Todd County, one of the state's smallest counties and one without a single stoplight. (The county was named for Colonel John Todd, another victim of the 1782 Battle of Blue Licks.) Robert Penn Warren, a poet and novelist who was born in Todd County, described Elkton as "a rather charming old town, not yet undone by time and progress."

For some authentic small-town atmosphere, stop in the South Forks restaurant on the courthouse square. Amish and

Mennonite farmers are an increasing presence in the area. The Amish Schlabach's Bakery, about ten miles south on KY 181, is a popular place for bread, sweet rolls, pies, cakes, and cookies.

Continue east on US 68 to Russellville, located in a valley among the knobs. (The town, first called Big Boiling Springs, was renamed to honor General William Russell of the Revolutionary Army.) In town, don't miss the classic Logan County Courthouse; an unusually large historic district, with many fine old houses, shade trees, and gardens; and the 1820 Bibb House, 183 West Eighth Street, built by a Revolutionary War officer whose son John developed Kentucky's distinctive Bibb lettuce in the 1850s.

The old Southern Bank Building, at the corner of Sixth and Main streets, was robbed by Jesse James and his gang in 1868; they wounded the bank president and escaped with $9,000. The building, now restored, is divided into apartments.

Russellville, considered one of the prettiest towns in the Pennyroyal area, is a good place for a stroll, and walking tour maps are available at 116 South Main on the public square. Antique shops abound. Early in October, highlights of the Logan County Tobacco Festival are a reenactment of the Jesse James robbery, tobacco jam, entertainment on the square, and a tour of homes.

Continue east on US 68 to South Union. From 1807 to 1922, members of the United Society of Believers in Christ's Second Appearing, commonly known as the Shakers, had a settlement in South Union. They built 200 buildings and owned more than 6,000 acres of land.

The Shakers, who believed in celibate, communal living separated from the temptations of "the world," were thrifty, industrious people, who set high standards for everything they did. At South Union, they farmed and raised livestock,

Shaker simplicity and elegance of design

operated a mill, tannery, and hat factory, sold their canned goods and preserves, and made silk from silkworms.

Now what remains is mainly the forty-room Centre House, built in 1824 and full of original Shaker furniture, crafts, tools, and equipment. It strikes the same chords as the much larger Shakertown at Pleasant Hill: simplicity, order, spare, elegant design, and a failed, but still touching, attempt to achieve a pure and selfless life.

Each bedroom has built-in fitted cabinets as well as wall pegs—the Shakers didn't like to leave things lying around. The many fireplaces were never used. Before the building was completed, the Shakers had developed a small, tidy cast-iron stove, a marvel of efficient design, that heated each room more cheaply and easily than a fireplace ever could.

Among the displays is an intriguing model of the Centre House, complete with miniature furniture and tiny dresses hanging from wall pegs. On the fourth floor, you'll find a bedroom with unusually fancy furnishings, such as a framed picture on the wall and a gramophone on a table—an indication that worldy influences were leaving their mark in the Shakers' later years.

One mile south, on KY 73, an old Shaker inn, built at a stagecoach stop to accommodate worldly travelers, has been restored and is now the Shaker Tavern, a bed and breakfast inn. Worldly travelers should like it here. The tavern stands in a grove of old trees, across the street—actually, a country lane—from the old Shaker post office. The pillared front porch faces old railroad tracks and a cornfield. It's an attractive place in a peaceful setting, only twelve miles from Bowling Green.

Continue on US 68 to Bowling Green. Bowling Green, Kentucky's fifth largest city, was established in 1798 along the Barren River. The town was captured by the Confederate Army in 1861, declared the Confederate capital of Kentucky until 1862, and survived other ups and downs through the years. Now it's flourishing; almost a boom town, some say. The home of Western Kentucky University, Bowling Green is a regional industrial and trade center and likely to become a tourism center as well, with Mammoth Cave, the Barren River

Visit Fat Man's Misery and the Bottomless Pit at Mammoth Caves

Lake State Resort Park, Shakertown at South Union, and other attractions nearby.

Visitors should see Fountain Square, an acre park in the center of town and the Kentucky Museum and Library on the Western Kentucky University campus. The GM Corvette Assembly Plant, one of the most highly computerized assembly plants in the world, has weekday tours *and* the National Corvette Museum.

Also in Bowling Green: the historic 1857 Hobson House, five historic districts listed on the National Register of Historic Places, a good selection of shops and restaurants, and traffic tie-up during rush hour.

Bowling Green has its share of underground streams, caves, and sinkholes, with their attendant problems, which the city is determined to work out. "It's one of the most bizarre landscapes on earth," said Kentucky Western professor Nick Crawford, an expert on karst terrain.

From Bowling Green, take I-65 northeast to Cave City (exit 53). Take KY 70 west to KY 255 and the entrance to Mammoth Cave National Park. Cave City is as far as you can get from the country-roads concept of traveling: all signboards, neon lights, flashing arrows, and promises of non-stop fun and entertainment. The Kentucky Action Park features an alpine slide ("¹/4 mile of excitement down a mountain of fun!"), go-carts, bumper boats, and a chair lift. Guntown Mountain has "20 free shows daily!" and staged gunfights in a Wild West town, amusement rides, a haunted house, and tours of Onyx Cave. There's a wax museum, a wildlife museum, rock shops, and miniature golf; factory outlet stores, a maze of motels, and fast-food restaurants. Wigwam Village has fifteen motel rooms in separate concrete wigwams, plus an Indian Gift Shop and Large Playground.

A strong commercial flavor has always been evident in the cave country, which first became famous in the 1820s. An

Indian mummy, found in another cave, was exhibited in Mammoth Cave as a tourist attraction. Then a man named Nathan Ward stole the mummy and went to Europe on a lecture tour with the "Mammoth Cave mummy"—and soon Mammoth Cave was better known in Europe than in many Kentucky towns.

During the early 1900s, twenty commercial caves competed fiercely for tourist attention. One was Crystal Cave, discovered in 1917 by a local farmer and cave explorer, Floyd Collins. He was exploring another cave on January 30, 1925, when he was trapped by a dislodged rock. Rescue efforts attracted national attention—even Charles Lindbergh showed up—and crowds of people gathered around the cave entrance. When rescue workers finally reached Floyd Collins on February 16, he was dead. The body was removed and buried in a family plot; two years later, against the family wishes, the body was exhumed and placed in a coffin inside Crystal Cave. The saga finally ended in 1961 when the National Park Service bought the cave and closed it to the public.

The commercial attractions of Cave City end well before the entrance to Mammoth Cave National Park, and the land becomes quiet, green, and dark with trees. You'll find 52,000 acres of protected forest lands for hiking and seventy miles of trails. There are sinkholes, too, and rivers. The Green River, winding through the park, provides canoe runs and cruises on the *Miss Green River II.*

But the park's major attraction is, of course, underground: the longest cave system in the world, with more than 300 miles of explored passageways. A variety of ranger-led tours are offered, all of them starting at the visitor center: to the Frozen Niagara, Fat Man's Misery, the Bottomless Pit, Crystal Lake, Grand Central Station. One tour includes lunch in the Snowball Dining Room, 267 feet below ground, where you sit at long utility tables and stare up at the formations above. Take a sweater. Summer temperatures in the caves stay at about 54 degrees.

Returning to Cave City, take US 32W northeast to Horse Cave. Or take I-65 north about five miles to exit 58. Horse Cave is an interesting little town with an unusual asset: a professional repertory theater group, the Horse Cave Theater, performing five plays on a rotating basis throughout the summer season. This means you can see three plays in two days; 1992's summer plays were *Panic in Paris*, a farce; *The Boys Next Door*, a comedy; *His First, Best Country*, an original play by a Kentucky author; Shakespeare's *The Tempest*; and *Sleuth*, a thriller.

This is no outdoor summer entertainment, but good professional theater. The air-conditioned theater seats nearly 350 people around a thrust stage; the lobby, designed to suggest a local tobacco-curing barn, displays the work of area artists.

We were in town on a sultry Monday night when no performance was scheduled. Walking past the theater, we heard rock music, laughter, and a sudden, theatrical scream. A rehearsal, I assumed. "Or a good party," Bill said.

In the beginning, the town took its name from the cave. Two stories explain how the cave was named. One has it that a band of horse thieves used the cave to hide stolen horses. The other claims that a horse fell into the cave. (And a pioneer said, "I know! Let's call it Horse Cave!") In any event, the town was also Horse Cave, in spite of a brief attempt to switch to the more stately name of "Caverna."

The cave's name was changed in 1916 when the cave was opened to the public and, it was thought, a better name was required; "Hidden River Cave" was the winner in a local cave-naming contest. Since then, it's been Horse Cave *and* Hidden River Cave. Take your pick. (We'll say Hidden River so you'll know when we're talking about the town.)

We were continuing our walk down Main Street in the summer twilight when Bill looked over a railing into what he assumed was a large stone quarry. Finding his way around the railing and junglelike growth of shrubs and vines, he slid down a muddy path to the bottom and saw the mouth of a large cave plunging under the shops on Main Street. Stairs, showing dimly in the twilight, dropped into darkness. He went down cautiously as far as the light held, felt cold air, and heard rushing water in the depths beyond. Welcome to Hidden River Cave!

As you will learn at the American Museum of Caves and Karstlands on East Main Street, the cave's history is an interesting one with a strong ecological message. In 1867 naturalist John Muir described the cave after a visit: "Arrived at Horse Cave, about 10 miles from the great cave [Mammoth Cave]. The entrance is by a long easy slope of several hundred yards. It seems like a noble gateway to the birthplace of springs and fountains and the dark treasuries of the mineral kingdom. This cave is in a village, which it supplies with an abundance of cold water, and cold air that issues from its fern-clad lips. In hot weather, crowds of people sit about it in the shade of the trees that guard it. This magnificent fan is capable of cooling everybody in the town at once."

Hidden River was shown as a tourist attraction from 1916 until 1943. It closed because, among other reasons, it had become the town sewer. According to a report written for the American Museum of Caves and Karstlands: "Hidden River Cave's pollution problem grew worse, and the cave's once abundant populations of blind cave fish and crayfish died out. By the 1970s, the odor of sewage emitting from the mouth of Hidden River Cave could be smelled throughout the downtown district." A happy ending is in the works. Horse Cave has a new sewage treatment system, the odor is gone, and the cave stream is "in the process of naturally renewing itself."

The cave is part of the American Museum of Caves and Karstlands, which provides an entrance to the cave and hopes to open the cave to the public in the summer of 1993. An elevator is being completed and stairs, permanent paths, and lights are being installed.

Horse Cave is appealing; you want the town to do well. A historic cave and good summer theater sound like a very promising combination.

From Horse Cave, take I-65 north to Louisville.

In the Area

All numbers are within area code 502.

Lake Barkley State Resort Park, Box 790, Cadiz, KY 42211-0790. Reservations: 1-800-325-1708.

Cadiz-Trigg County Tourist Commission, P.O. Box 735 TG, Cadiz, KY 42211. 522-3892.

Broadbent's Food & Gifts, US 68 & I-24 (exit 65). 235-5294 or 1-800-841-2202.

Hopkinsville-Christian County Tourism Commission, 1209 S. Virginia St., P.O. Box 1382, Hopkinsville, KY 42241. 1-800-842-9959.

Crockett's Restaurant, 317 E. Main St. Lunch served weekdays, 11:00 a.m.-2:00 p.m.; dinner served Monday through Saturday, 5:00-10:00 p.m. 885-0944.

Pennyroyal Area Museum, 217 E. Ninth St. Open Tuesday through Friday, 9:00 a.m.-5:00 p.m.; Saturday, 10:00 a.m.-3:00 p.m. 887-4270.

Trail of Tears Commemorative Park. 886-8033.

Jefferson Davis Monument State Historic Site, P.O. Box 10, Fairview, KY 42221-0010. 886-1765.

South Forks Restaurant, Elkton, KY 265-5717.

Schlabach's Bakery, Elkton, KY 265-2075.

Logan County Chamber of Commerce, 116 S. Main St., Russellville, KY 42276. 726-2206.

Shakertown at South Union, KY 42283. 542-4167. Open daily April 1 through November 1, 9:00 a.m.-5:00 p.m.; Sunday, 1:00-5:00 p.m.

The Shaker Tavern, South Union, KY 42283. 542-6801.

Bowling Green/Warren County Tourist/Convention Commission, P.O. Box 1040 KTG, Bowling Green, KY 42102. 782-0800.

GM Corvette Assembly Plant, I-65, exit 28. Tours Monday through Friday, 9:00 a.m. and 1:00 p.m. 745-8419.

National Corvette Museum, I-65, exit 28. Monday through Friday, 10:00 a.m.-4:00 p.m. 781-7973.

Kentucky Museum and Library, Western Kentucky University, Tuesday through Saturday, 9:30 a.m.-4:00 p.m.; Sunday, 1:00-4:00 p.m. 745-2592.

Hobson House at Hobson Grove, 1100 W. Main St., Hobson Grove Park. Guided tours, Tuesday through Saturday, 10:00 a.m.-12:00 noon, 1:00-4:00 p.m.; Sunday, 1:00-4:00 p.m. 843-5565.

Barren River Lake State Resort Park, 1149 State Park Rd., Lucas, KY 42156-9709. Reservations: 1-800-325-0057.

Kentucky Action Park and Guntown Mountain Amusement Park, off I-65, exit 53, Cave City, KY. 773-3530.

Wigwam Village, I-65, exit 53. 773-3381.

Mammoth Cave National Park. Open every day but Christmas. Call 758-2251 or 758-2328 for information.

Horse Cave Theater, P.O. Box 215, Horse Cave, KY 42749. July 3 through November 1. 786-2177 or 1-800-342-2177.

The American Museum of Cave and Karstlands, Main St., P.O. Box 409, Horse Cave, KY 42749. 786-1466.

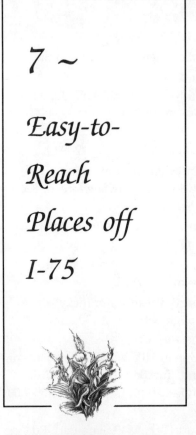

7 ~

Easy-to-Reach Places off I-75

Take I-75 and enough time to explore some country roads.

Highlights: *a historic farm, mansion, fort, pottery and mining camp; the Kentucky Horse Park, Keeneland Racetrack, bluegrass towns; the mighty Cumberland Falls; and a chance to buy an overpriced dulcimer.*

I-75, a major traffic artery, runs north and south through Kentucky. Crossing the Ohio River, it passes Covington, skirts Lexington, cuts through the Daniel Boone National Forest—which appears on Kentucky road maps as a swath of green spreading southward—emerges at London, then continues on to Tennessee.

This is all many interstate drivers have ever seen of Kentucky—motel and fast-food clusters, horse trailers, limestone cliffs, farms, green valleys and hills, isolated houses, outcroppings of coal, weathered shacks, and mountains. "Someday,

I'm going to take the time to see something of Kentucky," people say as they drive through.

Consider the following stops when you have some extra time—an hour or two, an afternoon, a day, even a weekend. Find a rest area off the interstate, meaning any place that sounds interesting. The natives are friendly and you can drink the water. There's very little risk involved. We did hear of a young man, just out of college, who was driving south on I-75 to a marketing job in Orlando, Florida. On an impulse, he decided to get off the road and have lunch in Berea. That was two years ago. Now he's a potter, living happily in Paint Lick.

The Dinsmore Homestead

The Kentucky flavor shows up early, about ten miles south of Covington, with a highway sign for Buttermilk Pike, and a water tower saying FLORENCE YALL!. Take KY 18 west to Burlington (about eight miles). The Dinsmore Homestead is 6.5 miles past Burlington, on the right, in hilly farmland.

James and Martha Dinsmore came to Kentucky and settled on this Boone County farm in 1842. They were a well-educated couple, originally from New England, not rich, but accustomed to a comfortable way of life. They had six slaves. The farm's major cash crops came from fruit orchards, corn and tobacco fields, and herds of sheep. Like many families in the area, the Dinsmores' loyalties were divided during the Civil War. James and Martha supported the Union, while their daughter Julia was engaged to a Confederate soldier, who was killed during the war. Julia Dinsmore inherited the farm after her father's death in 1872. She raised two nieces and kept a daily diary—filled with details of her struggles to keep the farm going—until her death in 1926.

If you're interested in turn-of-the century farm life, American history, or old houses in an untouched natural setting, don't miss the Dinsmore Homestead. It offers a vivid picture of one family's history—a history told through their house and possessions and thirty surrounding acres of the farm, as well as 90,000 pages of personal papers and documents.

The house is not made of logs, as you might expect, but is a spacious building, conventional in design, one that wouldn't look out of place in a Louisville suburb. It has a modest Greek Revival entrance and, at the back, a long porch. Among the outbuildings are a barn, a wine house, and a cookhouse in use until 1916, when a kitchen wing was added to the main house, along with plumbing and electricity.

Walk past the wine house and up a hill to see the family graveyard, enclosed by a low stone fence and sheltered by majestic walnut trees. All but one of the gravestones are of local limestone; the largest, a granite shaft, marks the grave of "Mammy," one of the slaves; her name, too, was Julia.

Inside the house, everything suggests that the Dinsmores just left and are expected back shortly. The dining room table is set for dinner; a turkey feather fan rests on the table. A moose head (given to Julia Dinsmore by Theodore Roosevelt) dominates the front hall.

The farm grounds are graced by large old trees: hickory, black walnut, tulip poplars. Behind the farm, the Nature Conservancy owns 109 acres of a climax forest. More Dinsmore farmland, across the road, is now owned by the county; it's to be open to the public as a "passive park," with picnic tables and nature trails.

Explore the hiking trails in the woods behind the house and a small gift shop in one of the outbuildings. Julia Dinsmore's diary and family documents are available on microfilm. Special events include a Harvest Festival in October and a Christmas party the first weekend in December. The Dinsmore Homestead is open from April to mid-December on Wednesday, Saturday, and Sunday, 1:00 p.m to 5:00 p.m., and to groups, artists, and scholars by appointment. The Dinsmore Homestead, P.O. Box 4533, Burlington, KY 41005; 606-586-6127/6117.

The home of future Derby winners

The Kentucky Horse Park

A few miles from the interstate, off exit 120, on Iron Works Pike and one of the area's most popular attractions for horse lovers, kids, and the curious, the park offers films, carriage and horseback rides, even a sleigh ride when there's snow. Also of interest are a walking farm tour, the International Museum of the Horse, and the Calumet Trophy Collection. Steeplechase racing, polo matches, and horse shows are held throughout the year. The park is open from 9:00 a.m. to 5:00 p.m. It is closed Monday and Tuesday from November 1 to mid-March as well as Thanksgiving, Christmas Eve and Christmas, New Year's Eve and New Year's Day. The Kentucky Horse Park, 4089 Iron Works Pike, Lexington, KY 40511; 606-233-4303.

The Keeneland Race Course

Take exit 115 to KY 4 (New Circle Road) west to US 60 (Versailles Road) and West to Keeneland (about fifteen miles). This is the only non-profit race track in the country, and generally considered to be a gem. A few hours here will give you the feeling of the bluegrass country as nothing else can. Meets take place in April and October. The Blue Grass Stakes, an important prep race for the Kentucky Derby, is an April highlight. Post time is 1:00 p.m. For information call 606-254-3412.

The Old Frankfort Pike to Midway and Georgetown

Take exit 115 to KY 4 (New Circle Road) west to KY 1681 (the old Frankfort Pike) northwest toward Midway. Take US 62 northeast into Midway and on to Georgetown. Return to I-75 at Georgetown. This tour of about thirty miles offers an easy look at the bluegrass countryside and two historic towns. (See tour 6 for details.) The usual lovely scenes occur: fabulous horse farms, flowering trees, old stone fences. The road passes "Airdrie Stud Horse Farm," owned by Kentucky Governor Brereton Jones, and "Lane's End," where England's Queen Elizabeth has been a visitor. (Some of her horses were boarded there, too.)

At Midway, the main attraction is historic Railroad Street and its many antique shops. For lunch, there's the Depot and the Horseman's Fodder Café, both on Railroad Street. Only the Café is open on Sunday. Customers who come from church and have the church bulletin handy get their drinks (coffee, tea, etc.) free.

At Georgetown, the 1820 Historic Breckinridge House, at 201 South Broadway, is a bed and breakfast inn, offering two suites and a lavish breakfast. 502-863-3163.

Fort Boonesborough State Park

Take Exit 95 to KY 627 northeast (about seven miles). Fort Boonesborough was Kentucky's second pioneer settlement, located near the Kentucky River and a salt lick that attracted herds of buffalo. In the spring of 1775, Daniel Boone and a company of thirty men set out to cut a road from the Cumberland Gap to the Kentucky River site, following first the Indian Warrior's Path, then buffalo roads and deer trails.

On the way, three men were killed in Indian attacks and others turned back, but Boone and what remained of his company made it to the Kentucky River and began building a fort. Fort Boonesborough was an important defensive settlement in Kentucky during the early pioneer days and survived frequent Indian attacks.

At the present Fort Boonesborough museum, a video presentation tells the story of those perilous days. One episode involves the capture of Daniel Boone's daughter and two other young women by Indians and their rescue, with Boone leading the rescue party. Another is the 1778 siege of Boonesborough when sixty men at the fort, along with a handful of women and children, withstood a ten-day siege by a large force of Shawnees under Chief Black Fish and French Canadians under English command. (It's said that Simon Kenton saved Boone's life during the siege.)

The replica of the fort, on a hill near the Kentucky River, offers daily craft demonstrations: pottery, toy making, weaving, candle making, a blacksmith at work. Most of the park activities are seasonal. Facilities include a playground, picnic area, miniature golf, a pool, and swimming in the river. Campsites are open year-round. Of special interest is the Kentucky Corps of Long-riflemen Interstate Invitational Tournament in early October. Fort Boonesborough State Park, 4375 Boonesborough Road, Richmond, KY 40475-9316; 606-527-3131.

The White Hall State Historic Site

Less than five miles off I-75, Winchester-Boonesborough exit, White Hall is a large (forty-four rooms!), imposing, and beautiful house, built in two parts. The first part was a one-story Federal brick house built in 1798 by Green Clay, a general in the Revolutionary War; the second part, an Italianate mansion, was completed in the 1860s for Clay's son, Cassius, who named it White Hall.

Cassius Marcellus Clay was a lawyer and fiery antislavery activist who became President Lincoln's ambassador to Russia. During the 1840s, Clay fought a duel and engaged in a bowie knife fight because of his antislavery views. White Hall was fortified to protect Clay and his antislavery newspaper, *The True American*, from attack. Still tempestuous in his eighties, Clay divorced his wife of forty-five years and married a teenage girl.

Now a picture of summertime serenity, White Hall contains period furniture, some of it original, and mementoes of the Clay family. You'll find a gift shop and picnic tables on the grounds. Special events include an antique car show in mid-May and a "Pops in the Park" concert by the Lexington Philharmonic orchestra in late August. White Hall State Historic Site, 500 White Hall Shrine Road, Richmond, KY 40475-0159. Open 9:00 a.m. to 5:30 p.m., April 1 to October 31; closed Monday and Tuesday after Labor Day. 606-623-9178.

Richmond

Take exit 90A off I-75. Richmond is a charming old town with a strong southern flavor, the home of Eastern Kentucky University and the scene of several Civil War battles. The Richmond Tourism Center, at City Hall on Main Street, provides a driving tour map of the Battle of Richmond (a companion audiocassette is available) and a walking tour map of historic homes and places on and around Lexington Avenue and Main Street. The 1849 courthouse was used as a hospital by both Union and Confederate forces during the Civil War. Two good downtown Main Street restaurants are Woody's (606-623-5130) and the Down Under (606-623-0305). Richmond Tourism Center, P.O. Box 250, Richmond, KY 40475; 606-623-1000.

Bybee Pottery, nine miles east of Richmond on KY 52, is the oldest pottery west of the Allegheny Mountains, established in 1809 by the Corneilison family, whose descendants are still in charge. Nothing much changes around here. The clays still come from a nearby clay mine known for its purity; designs and methods of production remain traditional. Bybee's pottery is very popular in Kentucky. Buyers start lining up at 7:00 a.m. for kiln firings at 8:00 a.m. on Monday, Wednesday, and Friday, and the day's production is usually sold out that morning.

The Moberly Grocery on Irvine Road (KY 52) near Bybee carries some pottery pieces if the Bybee salesroom is sold out when you show up. Or try the Crackerbarrel, just off I-75 at exit 90A. The Bybee salesroom and workshop are open on weekdays from 8:00 a.m. to noon and from 12:30 to 4:30 p.m. 606-369-5350.

Berea

Forty miles from Lexington, off exit 77, you enter Berea, the "Folk Arts and Crafts Capital of Kentucky," and also prime antiques territory. The town's Welcome Center, with bro-chures and information, is located in a 1920 train depot just one mile from I-75. The usual procedure is to start here to get an idea of the shops and studios you'd like to visit, and then go on to Berea College and its Boone Tavern Hotel, on the corner of Main and Prospect streets, to have lunch and plan your shopping or browsing strategy. Otherwise you might be lost for several days—Berea shops can be beguiling.

Traditional craft items predominate—no surprise there—but some contemporary designs in pottery, hand-woven cloth, furniture, and so on, are showing up. (We recall a wood wall clock, curiously shaped and painted orange and purple, that would attract attention anywhere.)

Berea College traces its origins to Cassius Clay, "the Lion of White Hall," who invited a fellow abolitionist, John Fee, to come to Madison County and start a school. Berea evolved from the one-room school Fee built in 1855 on land donated by Cassius Clay; its original mission was to educate former slaves and poor children from Appalachia. Berea College charges no tuition and requires all students to work in a col-lege industry while attending school. Students make up about 80 percent of the Boone Tavern Hotel staff.

It's said that Boone Tavern was built at the suggestion of the wife of a president of Berea College, after she had entertained 300 guests in one year. The tavern features such southern dishes as plantation ham, spoon bread, Jefferson Davis pie, and a dish described as Chicken Flakes in a Bird's Nest. Most of the hotel furniture was made by students. The Boone Tavern Gift Shop displays a variety of craft items: toys, baskets, brooms, ceramic and wrought iron pieces, and furniture.

The college's Appalachian Museum is on Jackson Street, behind the Tavern. Special events in Berea include a Ken-tucky Guild of Artists and Craftsmen Fair in the spring (mid-May) and the fall (early October) and a Celebration of

Traditional Music Festival, held on the last weekend in October. The Boone Tavern Hotel: 606-786-9358. Boone Tavern: 1-800-366-9358. Berea Welcome Center, P.O. Box 556, Dept. KG-92, Berea, KY 40403; 606-986-2540.

Lancaster

Take KY 595 west to KY 52 west. Shoppers and antique hunters, if not exhausted in Berea, may want to visit this farm town about twenty-five miles to the west. Settled in 1798 by pioneers from Lancaster, Pennsylvania, Lancaster has an 1868 Victorian courthouse and a claustrophobic old jail now used as a historical museum and meeting place. "It's sort of interesting, as long as you know you can get out," a visitor remarked. More to the point, Lancaster has antique shops, notably, the vast (20,000 square feet) Lancaster Antique Market, which attracts buyers from as far away as California.

In the last few years, Lancaster has added a city-wide yard sale on August 22, which has been a big success. Last year's event attracted about 3,000 visitors.

Outside of town, the Carry A. Nation Birthplace is on Fisherford Road, near Harrington Lake. Carry's hatred of liquor stemmed from a wretched marriage to an alcoholic doctor, who was drunk at their wedding and stayed that way. He died shortly after Carry left him, and, history relates, Carry blamed his death on tobacco, booze, and the Masonic Lodge. (She was married to her second husband and living in Medicine Lodge, Kansas, when she began her career of smashing up saloons.) For information, contact the Garrard County Chamber of Commerce, P.O. Box 273, Lancaster, KY 40444; 606-792-2282.

Corbin

Take exit 29. Go south on US 25 one mile, then right on US 25W one-half mile. This brings you to the Harlan Sanders Café & Museum (see chapter 9), birthplace of the original fried chicken recipe (Colonel Sanders used a pressure cooker to speed up the process) and the subsequent Kentucky Fried Chicken empire. There are interesting exhibits and memorabilia of the only-in-America kind. A gleaming Kentucky Fried Chicken outlet is handy for lunch. (You were expecting Pizza Hut?) City of Corbin Tourist and Convention Commission, 101 N. Lynn Avenue, Corbin, KY 40701; 606-528-6390.

Cumberland Falls State Resort Park

Take the Corbin exit (29) to US 25W and KY 90. The distance to the park is about thirty miles. Once off the interstate, the road quickly leads into mountain country, the Daniel Boone National Forest, and some stunning mountain scenery: a wild river, a thundering waterfall that produces one of the only two "moonbows" in the world, and an old mining town.

The Cumberland Falls park, open all year, offers rooms in the Dupont Lodge, cottages and seasonal campsites, as well as seasonal pleasures such as seventeen miles of hiking trails, horseback riding, river and lake fishing, canoeing, river rafting, a pool, and a tennis court.

The sight and sound of the falls has a hypnotic effect as 10,000 gallons of water per second crash against rock. You stop to watch for a few minutes and find that half an hour has gone by. Pay attention to the warning signs around the falls and don't move too close. A teenage girl was killed a few years ago. She was dabbling her feet in the water, stood up, slipped on a mossy rock, fell in the water, and was swept over the falls. "The body wasn't found for a month," our informant said.

The waterfall—60 feet high and 120 feet wide, known as the "Niagara of the South"—plunges into a gorge littered with boulders. And other litter, sad to say. A marker near the falls explains: "Unfortunately, the wild Cumberland river has become a carrier of some of the waste that has been carelessly disposed of by Kentuckians who live upstream. . . . The natu-

ral currents and eddies formed around the boulders below
the falls act as traps for numerous plastic containers, dry
wood and other debris that are washed over the falls. As the
river level goes down, an unsightly social message is left for
all to see."

Still, the falls are a wonderful sight. We didn't try to
see the moonbow, a milky white arc that begins at the base
of the falls and ends downstream, because of the rainy spring
weather. The moonbow usually occurs around 1:00 a.m. on
clear nights when the moon is full; cold winter skies are sup-
posed to create the most beautiful moonbows, shining with
delicate colors.

We were at the park during a Nature Photography Shoot-
out Weekend, which meant that the area was full of energetic
people carrying tripods and cameras. They showed up everywhere: on top of cliffs, in the woods, perched precariously on
a rocky ledge, peering out beneath bushes. A husband and
wife photography team told us that they had seen and success-
fully photographed a moonbow. "Such a thrill, because you
know how rare it is. But we couldn't really see the colors until
we developed the film. It takes a five-to-six minute exposure."

A 1.5-mile park trail (#9) offers some of the best views of
the Cumberland Falls and leads to Eagle Falls, a waterfall so
sacred to the Indians of this area that they guarded it day and
night and fought a battle trying to keep it.

Other trails lead to Yahoo Falls and a small, scenic waterfall with the memorable name of Dog Slaughter. Not far away
is a natural scenic area, starring one of the state's largest sandstone arches. And, in the isolated and mountainous Big South
Fork National River and Recreation Area, is a reconstructed
coal mine and museum at Blue Heron.

You can take a sightseeing train (the Big South Fork
Scenic Railway) from Stearns to Blue Heron and back. It's a
three-hour trip, including time at Blue Heron. The train follows the coal company's tracks, cutting through mountain

country, crossing a trestle, passing old coal camps, and chugging through a tunnel blasted through solid rock.

Or you can drive, as we did. Take US 27 south to Stearns and KY 741 southwest to Blue Heron. The views are dramatic—mountains, boulders, forest, a gorge cut by a rushing river.

Blue Heron was a working coal mine employing over 200 people, then a ghost town. Now it's part of the National Park Service; the old train depot is used as a mining museum, with the company store, bathhouse, schoolhouse, and church down the road. There's a fishing lake stocked with catfish, and six campsites.

One of many interesting exhibits mentions "the noisy, dusty rattle of the tipple." You can see the rebuilt tipple, looking like a giant outdoor sculpture in the quiet, well-kept parkland. It's haunting, like the grimy, weary faces of the miners in museum photographs.

At the start of a trail leading to the old mining camp, a sign warns of copperheads and timber rattlesnakes in the woods: "Keep in mind it is against the law to kill a snake that has not threatened you."

Keeping that in mind, we decided not to take the trail.

Big South Fork Scenic Railway trains to Blue Heron depart from Stearns at 11:00 a.m. on weekdays and at 11:00 a.m. and 3:00 p.m. on weekends during the tourist season. For information, call 1-800-GO ALONG.

Williamsburg

Just off exit 11, eleven miles north of the Tennessee border, Williamsburg would like to be known as an "ideal halfway stop between Ontario and Florida." Whether or not that works out, it's a pleasant town where people nod and say hello to strangers walking by. It's also the birthplace of actress Patricia Neal and the home of Cumberland College, "Aunt

Julia Marcum" (a Civil War heroine; see the appropriate historical marker), and Beth Bates, the first girl in Kentucky to score in a high school football game. (She was playing for Williamsburg High School in 1982.)

Williamsburg is also where you'll find a big, cinderblock, no-frills country store called Bailey's, and the Bailey's Country Store Radio Show. The show is a local institution, heard on WCTT from 8:30 a.m. to 9:00 a.m. every day except Wednesday and Sunday, and offering a quick mix of country, gospel, and bluegrass music, weather and fishing reports, jokes, comments, and items for sale or trade. Sample item: "Man wants to give away a watchdog. Will bite but good with children. See Rick Helton in Owens Hollow in the red house."

Bailey's is located on Tenth Street, close to the interstate. Customers get free stovepipe and fishing advice, and they can help themselves from a lettuce, radish, and turnip patch by the store. This is the place for washboards, slop jars, lard buckets, belts for old treadle sewing machines, oilcloth, homemade quilts, and nuts and bolts for a horse-drawn plow. And more, much more, including "fiddles, guitars, dulcimers, and kazoos, all only slightly overpriced," according to owner Joe Bailey. He's willing to sell or trade anything, he says. "We sold a vault for a coffin once. Somebody bought it to put night crawlers in."

Bailey's has twice-weekly jam sessions in the store—bluegrass and country music on Mondays and Thursdays, from 5:00 p.m. to 8:00 p.m.—and occasional "acoustic anything" evenings. If all this makes Wal-Mart look a little inadequate, that's most likely the idea. Williamsburg Welcome Center, P.O. Box 2, Williamsburg, KY 40769; 606-549-0530 or 1-800-552-0530. Bailey's Store, Tenth Street, Williamsburg; 606-549-1822.

8 ~

Following US 68:

The Historic Buffalo Trace

Take US 68 from Maysville to Perryville then continue on roads to Bardstown and Louisville.

Highlights: *Maysville, Washington, a Revolutionary War battlefield at Blue Licks, the bluegrass country around Paris and Lexington, Shakertown at Pleasant Hill, a pioneer fort at Harrodsburg, a Civil War battlefield at Perryville, a brief look at Kentucky's Lincoln Country, a historic distillery, a Trappist monastery, and Stephen Foster's Bardstown.*

First the river, then the road. The Ohio served as the settlers' first highway. Coming ashore at Limestone Landing (later Maysville), they found a buffalo trail winding up the hill to Washington and on to Blue Licks, twenty-five miles inland on the banks of the Licking River and beyond. The settlers used such trails as the Indians had before them, finding that the migrant buffalo, moving fast in large herds, had chosen the easiest and most direct routes between watering holes and salt licks.

The Buffalo Trace, one of Kentucky's most historic roads, is now US 68. Beginning in Maysville, it runs southwest in an irregular line, roughly dividing the state in half. This tour follows US 68 from its beginning at Maysville to Perryville, then continues on other roads to Bardstown and on to Louisville, approximately 181 miles.

See Maysville and Washington (tour #5). Leaving Maysville on US 68 south, make a point of noticing that you're going up a hill. The three-mile journey from Maysville to Washington was an all-day struggle in pioneer times. Even in the late 1800s, it meant nearly an hour of strenuous effort. There's a story about a Maysville man who was courting a girl in Washington; after driving his horse and buggy up the hill, he arrived worn out, with this opening line: "I knew you were an angel, but I didn't know you resided in heaven!"

From Washington, continue south to Blue Licks. It makes a difference, driving along this pleasant, easy road, to think about early travel on the Buffalo Trace (or Smith's Wagon Road, as it was known in honor of the first man to cover the entire sixty-five miles from Maysville to Lexington in a horse-drawn wagon). First, there was the danger of Indian attacks. Later, the road was paved with logs covered by a layer of soil—an improvement in dry weather, but a bone-crushing rough ride when rain washed the soil away. Stagecoaches often overturned and horses went lame. After the road was hard-surfaced in the 1830s, another hazard appeared: the payment of tolls every four or five miles. A man on horseback was charged a quarter, and a horse and buggy driver 50 cents at every tollhouse.

Back to the present: Local people say that several small houses near May's Lick, easily seen from the road, could be pioneer log cabins covered with layers of tar paper or siding. "One way you can tell is that the chimney is built separately on the side of the house. And the roof has a swag and a steep pitch."

Blue Licks Battlefield State Park is the site of what is usually called "the last battle of the American Revolution" on

August 19, 1782. In fact, this battle was only one of many frontier clashes between Americans and British-led Indians that occurred between the 1781 defeat of the British army at Yorktown and the final peace agreement in 1783. The fight began when an Indian force led by a Canadian captain attacked Bryan's Station, an outpost near Lexington. After a two-day siege, the Indians withdrew and moved north. Aroused by news of the attack, Kentucky militiamen formed a regiment and set out in pursuit. The two forces came within striking distance at the Licking River near Blue Licks. Daniel Boone, knowing the countryside, feared an ambush. He advised waiting for reinforcements or using diversionary tactics. But a few hotheads impulsively rode their horses across the river, yelling war whoops, and the others had to follow . . . up and over a hill, straight into an ambush. It was a rout. Nearly seventy Americans were killed, including Boone's son, Israel. Another son, although wounded, escaped.

A granite shaft near the park entrance is inscribed with an improbable quote from Daniel Boone: "So valiantly did our small party fight that, to the memory of those who unfortunately fell in the battle, enough honor can not be paid." Taking part in the battle were 182 Americans and 240 Indians and Canadians. The American officers killed or captured are listed, followed by the privates killed or captured, and those who escaped. Among all the Anglo-Saxon names, one exception stands out: Anthony Sandusky. The unnamed Indians come last, in a poetic-sounding list: "Wyandots and Mingoes, Ottawas and Chippewas, Shawnees and Delawares."

The park has a small museum, a pool, hiking trails, cottages, seasonal camping sites, and a nature preserve. A very rare plant, Short's Goldenrod, is found here and nowhere else. "It grows along the rocky glade openings and a remnant of the buffalo trace that once led to the salt licks." A reenactment of the Battle of Blue Licks is held in mid-August.

We picnicked in a grove of trees near the museum and the site of the 1782 ambush. It was an autumnal Saturday afternoon, and a high school football game was in progress not far away; the fierce yells and fight chants sounded like echoes from the battle of long ago.

Continuing southwest on US 68 toward Paris, eight miles south of Blue Licks, look for the stone fences and rolling meadowland of Forest Retreat Farm. The main house, on the right, was built in 1820 by Thomas Metcalfe, a Kentucky governor and senator who began his career as a stone mason and was known as "Old Stone Hammer." The one-story building on the left, now a farm outbuilding, was once the Forest Retreat Tavern, a stagecoach stop marking the midway point between Maysville and Lexington when the trip took two days.

Thomas Metcalfe was instrumental in having the Maysville-Lexington Pike macadamized in 1830, "and therefore it was no coincidence that the road ran immediately past his house rather than through the county seat of Carlisle, three miles to the east," Dr. Taylor Asbury wrote. "A beautifully constructed road, it remained essentially unchanged for well over 100 years."

Note: Carlisle's courthouse square features an "intact nineteenth-century commercial district; all 350 buildings are on the National Register of Historic Places. There's also a log cabin said to be Daniel Boone's last Kentucky home.

Suggested side trip: About ten miles south of Blue Licks, KY 32, a winding two-lane road, leads west through rich farmland to Cynthiana, an out-of-the-way, old bluegrass town. We went through a village called Headquarters, passed several Charolai cows ambling down the middle of the road and saw a blue heron wading in a creek. The Indian Creek Baptist Church appears on the left, outside of Cynthiana. One of the first churches built west of the Allegheny Mountains, it was in continual use until 1965. Revolutionary War soldiers are buried in the churchyard. Cynthiana's white brick Harrison County courthouse, built in 1853, contains papers of Henry Clay. Just behind is the 1790 log courthouse where Clay once practiced law. It's now the headquarters of a radio station, WCYN.

Return to US 68 on KY 32. (Or take US 62 south to George-town.) US 68 toward Paris is called the Paris Pike. Around here you begin to see the famous horse farms of the bluegrass county: horses and foals out to pasture, acres of lush green pastureland, avenues of trees leading back to impressive houses. And fences—stone fences, black or white rail fences—marking off the land like the bold strokes of an artist's brush.

Paris is in the heart of the bluegrass. A welcoming sign says it all: "Horses, History, Hospitality." The town, established in 1789, was first called Hopewell. According to one account, it was another stopoff point between Maysville and Lexington, and wagoners were wont to say, "Hope we'll get there before night." The name was changed to Paris, and the county called Bourbon, in gratitude for French help during the Revolutionary War. The center of Paris is the attractive square built around the Bourbon County Courthouse. Old records show several suits for debt against Daniel Boone, living in Maysville, and Simon Kenton, in Washington. Both towns were then part of Bourbon County.

The Duncan Tavern, like the adjacent Anne Duncan house, was built of limestone in 1788. It was the main stopping place for travelers on the Maysville-Lexington stagecoach run, and the first Kentucky tavern to sell bourbon. Both Boone and Kenton stopped by in the tavern's rough and rowdy days. Now the restored building is furnished with antiques, and is a model of good taste and decorum.

Paris has some interesting shops—and drive-in liquor stores. Loch Lea Antiques, 410 Main Street, has a good selection of old Kentucky folk art.

The Cane Ridge Shrine, outside of Paris on KY 537, is a 1791 pioneer log church protected by a limestone superstructure, and the founding church of the Disciples of Christ. Originally the church was Presbyterian. When the Great Revival of 1800 swept through Kentucky, one of the largest and most famous revival meetings was held at Cane Ridge. A crowd of 30,000 gathered outside in the light of torches and listened to five or six men preaching simultaneously for hours. In a frenzy of religious fervor, people began to sing, shout, sob, speak in tongues, and fall into trances. All this was taken as evidence of salvation.

Paris is the site of the Bourbon County Fair and Saddlehorse Show held during the last week in July. If you'd like to tour a horse farm, try calling Claiborne Farms (606-987-2330) or Stone Farm (606-987-3737) to set up an appointment.

Continue on US 68 through Lexington. Approaching Lexington, you see even larger and more opulent horse farms, scenes that may lead to delightful daydreams about the country gentry life, replete with private planes, houseguests, and elegant dinner parties. This is a rich area, in more ways than one, and there's much to see and do in and around Lexington—plenty of antique shops, of course, and a boutique for horse lovers called Rags 'n Nags.

The Keeneland Race Course, six miles west on Versailles Road, US 60, has thoroughbred racing in April and October. Keeneland means racing at its most traditional and appealing: a country setting, flowers, shade trees, a fieldstone grandstand, and a stylish crowd. You can watch the horses being saddled under the trees before they're brought into the walking ring. Incidentally, the track will provide parasols for ladies who want protection from the sun.

Three suggested side trips: 1. The Kentucky Horse Park, off I-75 (see chapter 7).

2. Georgetown, north of Lexington off I-75, is the home of Georgetown College, founded in 1829, and the first Japanese-owned plant in the United States, located appropriately on Cherry Blossom Way. The huge Toyota plant is automated and touring visitors will see robots welding auto bodies.

Look for a historic marker on the corner of Main and Water streets, just before a bridge. To the left, you'll see a small park, a log cabin, and a stream. It's easy to miss. The first marker reads, "Royal Spring: One of the finest in Kentucky, discovered July 9, 1774, by Colonel John Floyd and party." It's still the source of Georgetown's water supply.

The second marker gets down to cases. "Birthplace of Bourbon: The Reverend Elijah Craig, founder of Craig's Classical School, first distilled bourbon whiskey on this site in 1789. A pioneer from Virginia, Reverend Craig set up his grain mill and used the fine limestone water of Royal Spring to develop the first sour mash process in the production of bourbon." Hailed as the founder of Georgetown, Reverend Craig also operated the "first fulling mill and paper mill west of the Allegheny mountains." A busy, and no doubt prosper-

Antiquers will love historic Railroad Avenue in Midway

ous, man. *Note:* Elijah Craig bourbon, a premium brand, is made in Bardstown.

3. Midway. For an especially scenic drive, take KY 1681, the old Frankfort Pike, west from Lexington to US 62 north to Midway. Old stone fences, magnificent horse farms, clouds of pink and white dogwood will delight you in the spring. Stop in at the unusual Headley-Whitney Museum (jeweled bibelots, a shell grotto, Oriental porcelains) along the way.

Midway is a railroad town, midway between Lexington and Frankfort, the state capital. Railroad tracks divide the busiest street, which is lined with shops in Victorian storefront buildings. Music plays from a loudspeaker as shoppers drift in and out of the antique and gift shops and take refuge in the Depot or the Horseman's Fodder Café for lunch. It's a cheerful scene.

In one antique shop, we asked the owner if most of the stock came from Kentucky. He looked amused. "Those days are long gone," he said. "It's an international market now. For example, we had a nice Amish quilt from Pennsylvania. After six months it went to a shop in Indiana. A lady from San Francisco bought it there and shipped it to a buyer in Japan."

Historical markers along Railroad Avenue tell of Morgan's Raiders hitting Midway during the Civil War and using the telegraph line to try and lure the train back to Midway so they could blow it up. But the railroad engineer at the other end failed to be convinced. Reading all this, you can easily picture the duel between two unseen adversaries, and hear a few ghostly chuckles. Is it possible that historical markers in Kentucky are more interesting than elsewhere? They speak with as many voices as people do.

There is, however, no marker relating the fact that former First Dog Millie, the spaniel owned by President and Mrs. George Bush, was bred here.

Midway College, Kentucky's only women's college, has a pretty campus, stables, a riding course, and a unique Equine Office Administration program. Its equitation (horseback) team ranks fifth in the nation.

Past Lexington, continue southwest on US 68 to Shakertown at Pleasant Hill—another lovely drive. The twisting road goes past a few suburban developments with names like Equestrian Estates, more horse farms, limestone cliffs, deep woods, with yellow and white daisies growing along the road. This was a Shaker toll road in the early 1800s.

The land becomes more open as the entrance to Shakertown approaches; you see cattle and sheep out in the meadows, tidy fences, groves of oak and walnut trees. It's time to forget the daydreams suggested by the opulent horse farms. The Shaker vision of the good life was very different: simplicity, hard work, celibacy, equality, and social justice in a communal life kept separate from "the carnal world."

The Shakers were pacifists and opposed to slavery; as early as 1819, they began buying and freeing slaves and offering them full brotherhood. "Shakers" was the familiar name for members of the United Society of Believers in Christ's Second Appearing and stemmed from the energetic dancing that was part of their worship service. The first Shaker settlement, at Shawnee Run, was moved to Pleasant Hill in 1809. By 1840, the Shakers—500 strong—had built 270 buildings, owned more than 4,000 acres, and were profitably trading their produce and goods with "the world."

The Shaker name was a guarantee of high quality in everything from garden seeds and silk to furniture. They invented the flat broom, the first hydraulic water system in Kentucky, the dumbwaiter in houses, and a miniature railway to carry feed to animals in the barn. Any work well done, they believed, was a prayer. They saw the beauty in humble objects: jars, boxes, a broom, a chair.

Their decline, which began in the 1850s, was accelerated by the Civil War. When the Battle of Perryville was fought near Harrodsburg, the Shakers carried supplies and provisions to the wounded. Soon they were feeding "300 to 1000 per day and night with thousands of others begging for a small bit to eat." By the end of the war, all the Shaker stores of food, livestock, wagons, and flatboats had been confiscated—a serious loss. New believers became scarce. The community dwindled away until, in 1923, it ceased to exist.

A remarkable preservation effort saved and restored thirty original buildings and 2,700 acres of Shaker farmland in a pastoral setting by the Kentucky River. This is Shakertown at Pleasant Hill today—a showcase of Shaker architecture, artifacts, and furniture and an American treasure.

Tours of the village are self-guided, and start on a high note with the splendid Centre Family Dwelling. "Interpreters," wearing Shaker dress, are stationed in each building to answer questions and tell the Shaker story. Look for the daily craft demonstrations, special events (cooking, chair making, sheep sheering, silk culturing), wildflower hikes, and sleigh rides in the snow. The old stern-wheeler *Dixie Belle* makes regular trips down the Kentucky River from April through November. Hiking trails lead through the remaining Shaker land.

Arriving late on a chilly September afternoon, we saw the spare, handsome Shaker buildings appear dreamlike in a heavy mist rolling in from the river: an enchanted village, like Brigadoon.

This is the only historic village in the country that offers guest rooms in the original buildings; we were in the brick West Family Building. Two polished wood stairways—the Shakers had one for the women, one for the men—led to a comfortable second-floor room furnished with rag rugs and reproductions of Shaker furniture, all in the characteristic colors of off-white, rose, and a smoky blue. There was no closet. Our clothes, hung on wooden pegs, looked surprisingly decorative against the white walls, and the room stayed neat. (Worldly amenities included air conditioning, telephone, TV, and a gleaming tiled bathroom.)

The dining room, serving Shaker specialties, is in the Trustees' Office. Eggs in aspic on anchovy toast, corn pudding, and lemon pie, made the Shaker way with thin slices of fresh lemon, are especially recommended. A group that had just finished singing Shaker hymns was filing out when we arrived. "Call me," one woman murmured to another. "I'm *desperate* for tenors."

Coming downstairs the next morning, looking for an early cup of coffee, I found a guest watching "With Hands and Hearts," a TV video on Shaker history narrated by Helen Hayes. She said: "I called my husband last night, and he said, 'How is it there?' 'Terrific!' I told him. 'You wouldn't believe it!' And he said, 'No clutter, right?' "

We both laughed at that. "I have three small children at home," she added, with a nice smile.

Most visitors feel, in one way or another, something of the Shaker spirit at Pleasant Hill. It inspires a desire to go home and get the clutter out of your house . . . even, if possible, your life.

" 'Tis a gift to be simple, 'tis a gift to be free, 'tis a gift to come down where you want to be," the Shakers sang in their best-known hymn. From a nineteenth-century description: "The streets are quiet; for here you have no grog shop, no beer house, no lock up, no pound . . . and every building, whatever may be its use, has something of the air of a chapel. The paint is all fresh; the planks are clean bright; the windows are all clean. A sheen is on everything; a happy quiet reigns."

Continue on US 68 to Harrodsburg. Harrodsburg Pottery and Crafts, one-half mile east of Harrodsburg, is surrounded by flowers and an herb garden. The shop carries local pottery, hand-dipped candles, and many Kentucky craft items such as honeysuckle baskets, rag rugs, and punched tin.

Harrodsburg is a friendly bluegrass town with a long history behind it. Founded by James Harrod in 1774, it was the first permanent English settlement west of the Alleghenies and is the oldest town in the state.

The Old Fort Harrod State Park has a replica of the fort, one-third smaller than the original, built around the spring that first attracted Harrod to the site. Admire the sheltering old osage orange tree near the fort entrance, and visit the amphitheater where *The Legend of Daniel Boone* is performed every summer and the Lincoln Marriage Temple, a stone chapel-like building containing the crude cabin where Abraham Lincoln's parents were married (maybe).

It's fun to tour the fort, especially with children. When we were there, a costumed guide in the blockhouse was working on quilt squares. Another guide was making baskets in the schoolhouse. Children were racing around outside, having a fine time. "Mom!" cried an indignant young voice. "It's my turn to be Daniel Boone and Jason won't be the Indians!"

In a world giddy with change, it's good to know a few places that stay the same. One of these is the Beaumont Inn in Harrodsburg. The stately Greek Revival building, built in 1845 as a school for young ladies, became an inn in 1918, owned and managed by the Dedman family, whose descendants are still in charge.

Inside the style is Victorian: flowered carpets, curtains of Brussels lace, and many Dedman family pieces among the antique furniture. "If some calamity occurred, we'd try to save two things first—great-grandmother's desk in the front hall, and, upstairs, the bed her nine children were born in," said Chuck Dedman, the manager. (The bed is in room 28.)

A dinner bell is rung before the evening meal. Because Mercer County is dry, a "Beaumont Cocktail" is a glass of ice water. BYOB. The dining room is famous for its hickory-smoked country ham, "yellow-legged fried chicken," and traditional southern dishes like spoon bread and General Robert E. Lee orange-lemon cake.

Breakfast is a soothing experience in decorous indulgence. A soft-spoken, motherly waitress appears immediately with coffee. The cornmeal batter cakes are a house specialty. Small, delicate, and tasty, they tend to disappear quickly. But the waitress will be glad to bring you more. She asks if you'd like more butter, syrup, strawberry jam—"And how's the coffee? Should I dump that out and pour you some fresh?"

After breakfast, it's good to take a walk around the grounds. Do you know a pawpaw tree when you see one, or a swamp cyprus, or a Kentucky coffee tree? The large gnarled tree near the inn's entrance might stump an expert; it's four trees—a catalpa, hackberry, wild cherry, and grapevine—grown together.

From Harrodsburg, take US 68 southwest to Perryville. We recommend a side trip on US 150 east to Danville, founded in 1783. It has many fine old houses, tree-lined streets, and the lively air of a college town. Centre College, established in 1819, has a handsome campus and one of the oldest administration buildings still in use.

The Great American Brass Band Festival, trumpets blaring, hits the Centre Campus in mid-June. The Constitution Square State Historic Site is on South Second Street, and the restored McDowell House and Apothecary Shop, where Dr. Ephraim McDowell, a pioneer surgeon, lived and practiced, is across the street.

From Danville or Perryville, head west on US 150 to Perryville Battlefield State Historic Site. The Elmwood Inn in Perryville is in a historic house that was used as a hospital during the Civil War battle. There's a restaurant serving lunch and dinner, as well as bed and breakfast rooms and afternoon tea.

The battlefield is about two miles outside of Perryville. (You'll know you're near when you see a barn advertising Battlefield Antiques.) Perryville has the somber distinction of being the site of one of the bloodiest battles of the Civil War— a battle that ended in a tactical victory for the South but an overall defeat. When the Confederate troops withdrew, their efforts to control Kentucky came to an end.

The date was October 8, 1862—a hot, dry day. Soldiers in both the Confederate and Union armies were desperate for water. Marching toward Perryville, a soldier of the 50th Ohio Volunteer Infantry wrote home that "the boys got some water out of a dark pond one night and used it to make their coffee . . . what was their disgust the next morning to find a dead mule or two in the pond. I imagine the coffee had a rich flavor." On the 7th of October, Confederate troops under General Braxton F. Bragg seized the nearly dried-out Doctor's

Creek near Perryville. In the afternoon, the creek was taken by advance cavalry of Union General Don Carlos Buell. On the morning of October 8, a battalion of Union soldiers more than three miles long faced an equal line of Confederate soldiers. The battle began at about 2:00 p.m. and raged until dark. Smoke and the sound of cannonfire reached Harrodsburg.

That night, when the cannons were silent, the cries of the wounded and dying men filled the air. Churches and farmhouses were commandeered for use as field hospitals. There were gruesome reports of surgeons operating all day in an upstairs room and the staircase filling up with amputated limbs. The final count of casualties: 8,000. A Union soldier wrote in a letter home: "The moon shone full upon the scene. . . . Oh, may you never see such a sight."

Stories are still told about the battle. Chuck Dedman, the Beaumont Inn manager, said that his wife's great-great-grandfather was thirteen years old at the time. Being young and curious, he rode a mule out to Perryville the next day to look around. "They say he didn't stay long. And he was sick all the way home."

Like many old battlefields, Perryville is a peculiarly peaceful place, full of shade trees and the sound of mockingbirds. There's a small museum. A Confederate monument stands near the site of one of the bloodiest charges. The Battle of Perryville is reenacted every year on the October weekend closest to the battle date.

"The battle started over water, and it's still hard to get a drink," a visitor noted, bending over a reluctant water fountain. The museum displays a letter from the Confederate General E. Kirby Smith, "The Kentuckians are slow and backward in rallying to our standard. Their hearts are with us, but their blue-grass and their fat-grass cattle are against us." In other words, Kentuckians preferred good living to ideology. It seems that they still do.

From Perryville Battlefield, take KY 150 west to Springfield. Springfield is the town where Nancy Hanks grew up and married Thomas Lincoln. Their son, Abraham, was born after the Lincolns had moved on, but Springfield is part of Kentucky's official Lincoln Country. The Lincoln Homestead State Park, five miles north of town, occupies land settled by the Lincoln family in 1782. It's thought that Abraham Lincoln's grandfather was killed by Indians somewhere around here. The log cabin where Nancy Hanks lived as a child is in the park, as well as a replica of Thomas Lincoln's boyhood cabin and a blacksmith shop where he worked. Adding to the ambiance is the eighteen-hole Lincoln Homestead Golf Course.

A re-enactment of Nancy Hanks's wedding is produced every June 13, and a Nancy Hanks Golf Tournament is held in May. (I'd like to picture the golfers in pioneer dress, but that probably is not the case.)

Springfield has more than the Lincoln connection. It's a nice town, often described as one of the prettiest in the state, and its Main Street is without a single vacant store—a noteworthy distinction, these days. The 1861 courthouse is still in use. Records dating back to 1792, include the Nancy Hanks-Thomas Lincoln marriage certificate.

Note: The Abraham Lincoln Birthplace National Historic Site is just south of Hodgenville on US 31E. Here the log cabin traditionally known as Lincoln's birthplace is enclosed in a monument made of Connecticut pink marble and Tennessee granite. The fifty-six steps leading to the monument represent the years of Lincoln's life. The grounds include a Visitors Center, 110 acres of the original Lincoln farm, and Sinking Spring, a limestone spring that supplied the family's water. (Steps lead to the spring for viewing.)

Lincoln's Boyhood Home at Knob Creek, seven miles north of Hodgenville on US 31E, features a replica of the cabin occupied by the Lincolns from 1811 to 1816. His earliest memories were of the Knob Creek farm, Abraham Lincoln said in later years. He and his sister, Sarah, went briefly to school at Knob Creek; a baby brother was born and died. Lincoln remembered a long day spent helping his parents plant corn and pumpkin seeds and watching the next day as a hard rain washed all the seeds away.

The Abraham Lincoln Birthplace has been one of the most visited shrines in the country since it opened in 1911. Still, there's room for differing views on how well this and other sites reflect the unpretentious man who was one of our greatest presidents. You must decide for yourself. To quote one irreverent visitor: "When you've seen one log cabin, you've pretty much seen 'em all."

From Springfield, take US 150 west to KY 152 west to KY 49. Go south on KY 49 to Loretto. A scenic, curving, hill-and-dale drive brings you to the small town of Loretto. Continue south another three miles and you'll see a sign that says, "You've just found the home of Maker's Mark." The only operating distillery that's a National Historic Landmark, Maker's Mark is a quaint nineteenth-century village of old buildings, most of them dark brown with red shutters, tucked into a small green valley and surrounded by hills. The original buildings made up Burk's Mill and Distillery, which began operations in 1805 and continued until closed by Prohibition.

In 1953 Taylor W. Samuels saw the abandoned, dilapidated buildings "with a stream running between them and a deep, cold, spring-fed lake on the hill above" and bought the whole 200-acre spread with the idea of making a premium whiskey: a corn and barley malt mix flavored with winter wheat, rather than the usual rye, and aged for six years in carefully rotated, charred white oak barrels. The result is a smooth, mellow bourbon that "works very well in a brandy

Whiskey by the barrel at Maker's Mark

snifter, but only for people who like to sip and savor. It's not for gulpers," said Bill Samuels, Jr., who's now in charge.

Guided tours are informative and entertaining. Our guide pointed out a handsome house on the hilltop where a yearly mint julep party is held at Derby time. "But don't feel bad if you didn't get an invitation," she said in a confidential tone. "You should see some of the guests who stay late, rolling down that hill."

In the old days of Burk's Mill and Distillery, local people brought jugs and jars to the Quart House to be filled on the spot from an open barrel. Today, Maker's Mark is forbidden by law to sell its product where it's made. You can, however, buy Maker's Mark in Loretto liquor stores.

The Toll Gate Shop has many MM mementoes for sale, including chocolate bourbon candy, creme de menthe mints, and a good bottled barbecue sauce. My husband, asking a clerk about the whiskey-making procedure, mentioned Jack Daniels and added jokingly. "If that isn't a forbidden word around here." The clerk, a regal redhead, was not amused. "It don't bother us none," she answered with a stony stare.

Note: There are various recipes for making a real Kentucky mint julep, with tiresome arguments about whether the mint should be bruised or crushed, the ice crushed or slivered, and so on. The best recipe probably came from the Louisville publisher Henry Watterson. Start with a coin silver goblet, he advised. "Dissolve one-half teaspoon of sugar in a spoonful of branch water. Take one fresh, tender mint leaf and crush it gently before dropping it into the sugar. Fill the goblet with cracked ice until it's frosted. Take a few more sprigs of mint and decorate the goblet's rim. Then pour at least four fingers of mellow Kentucky bourbon into another coin-silver goblet. Throw the other stuff away and drink the bourbon."

From Loretto, take KY 52 west to KY 247 (known locally as Monks Road) north toward Culvertown. Gethsemane is four miles north of Culvertown. Watch for a blinking light at the top of a hill—there's no sign—and turn right. The Gethsemane Farms Trappist Monastery is the oldest monastery west of the Allegheny Mountains, a secluded place of work and prayer for monks who belong to the ancient Order of Cistercians of the Strict Observance. The monastery was made famous by Thomas Merton, a monk there for twenty-seven years and author of the autobiographical *The Seven-Storey Mountain*. Thomas Merton is buried in the cemetery behind the retreat house, his grave marked by a small white cross inscribed "Fr. Louis Merton" and stating the dates of his birth and death.

Visitors have always been welcomed at Trappist abbeys. At Gethsemane, you can attend church services, which are held seven times a day, or follow a path in the "non-monastic" grounds across Monks Road where the Order owns 1,000 acres of meadows and woodland. If you find yourself thinking of the Shakers at Pleasant Hill, there's a connection. Thomas Merton liked Shakertown and visited there several times. The Shakers' belief in God, he wrote, showed in everything they made.

The monks at Gethsemane Farms operate a flourishing business making fruitcakes, cheese, and (a recent addition) bourbon chocolate candy. There's no gift shop.

Reservations for rooms (private, with shower) at the retreat house can be made by individuals or groups. Usually there's a waiting list. The first full week of each month is set aside for women; the rest of the month is for men. There's no set charge; offerings are made on an individual basis, according to each person's ability to pay. Those who have made retreats at Gethsemane speak of peace, serenity, and a feeling of renewal. Others have reported details: the beauty of the woodland paths, the chanting of the monks echoing in the church, the small cabin in the woods that was Thomas Merton's hermitage; worn jogging shoes showing below monkish robes, a cheerful monk in the bakery carrying a coffee cup with the motto "Get Even . . . Give Fruitcake!" and a bumper sticker, "Grace happens."

From Gethsemane, take US 31E northeast to Bardstown. Bardstown, one of the oldest cities in the state, has all the usual charms of old Kentucky towns: wide streets, splendid trees, handsome old houses, gardens, a historic courthouse square. It's also an unabashed tourist town, the "bourbon capital of the world," and a lot of fun if you're in the right mood.

Wickland, an 1819 Georgian house full of fine furniture and the former home of three governors, is well worth a visit. So is the 1816 St. Joseph's Cathedral, with paintings donated by Pope Leo XII. (Some guides prefer the legend that the paintings were gifts from the French King Louis Philippe.) You can take a carriage ride around town, visit a whiskey museum, a miniature soldier museum, the Old Bardstown Village and Civil War Museum and take the My Old Kentucky Home Dinner Train.

The old jail is now the Jailer's Inn, "completely renovated and decorated with heirlooms and antiques." It's a pleasant place to stay, as are the Bruntwood Inn Bed and Breakfast and Kenmore Farms.

Bardstown also has a monument to John Fitch, who invented the steamboat in 1791. The invention failed to make him happy. "I know of nothing so vexatious to a man of feeling," he wrote in his journal, "as a turbulent wife and steamboat building."

My Old Kentucky Home State Park is built around Federal Hill, an 1818 brick plantation house that is considered to be one of the best examples of Georgian Colonial architecture in the state. It was owned by John Rowan, a cousin of Stephen Foster's. According to legend, Federal Hill was what Foster was thinking about when he composed the song that begins, "Oh, the sun shines bright on my old Kentucky home." Guides in hoopskirts will point out the desk where Foster sat to write when inspiration struck.

During the summer, *The Stephen Foster Story* is presented nightly (except Mondays) in the park "under the stars." The heartwarming musical had its thirty-fourth season in 1992, and it's still going strong, with over 300 captivating costumes and dozens of Foster's most beloved songs. Well, you get the idea. It's a very popular show.

Stephen Foster is known to have visited Louisville and Augusta, Kentucky, with his mother when he was six years old. Beyond that, the record is cloudy. He may have visited Federal Hill in 1852, as some insist, but that was nine years after Judge Rowan's death and the son who inherited Federal Hill was in Europe. Foster's brother always said that "My Old Kentucky Home" was written in Pittsburgh. The widow of John Rowan, Jr., recalled, many years later, the very scene: Stephen Foster, a guest of her husband's, sat down in the hallway of Federal Hill and wrote the song as slaves sang and strummed on banjoes outside the window.

Does it matter? Not only is there controversy about when and why the song was written, there's trouble with the lyrics. (" 'Tis summer, the darkies are gay.") The answer may be to play the melody and forget the lyrics. That's what happens every year in Louisville at Derby time when the horses line up at the starting gate and the band plays "My Old Kentucky Home." It's a magical moment and Kentuckians—for all kinds of indefinable reasons—have tears in their eyes.

In the Area

All numbers are within area code 606.

Blue Licks Battlefield State Park, P.O. Box 66, Mount Olivet, KY 41064-0066. 606-289-5507.

Carlisle Visitors Center, Old Nicholas County Jail, 121 W. Main St., Carlisle, KY 40311. 289-5174.

Cynthiana/Harrison County Chamber of Commerce, P.O. Box 296, Cynthiana, KY 41031. 234-5236.

Paris-Bourbon County Chamber of Commerce, 2 Bank Row, Paris, KY 40361. 987-3205.

Cane Ridge Shrine, US 460 east to Cane Ridge Rd.,
    KY 537. Open weekdays, 9:00 a.m.-5:30 p.m.; Sunday,
    1:30-5:30 p.m.

Greater Lexington Convention and Visitors Bureau,
    Suite 363, 430 W. Vine St., Lexington, KY 40507.
    1-800-84-LEX-KY.

Keeneland Race Course. Meets in April and October; post
    time, 1:00 p.m. 254-3412.

Kentucky Horse Park, 4089 Iron Works Pike, Lexington, KY
    40511. 233-4303. Open daily, March 16-Oct. 31, 9:00 a.m.-
    5:00 p.m.; Nov. 1-March 15, Wednesday through
    Sunday, 9:00 a.m.-5:00 p.m.

Toyota Motor Manufacturing, USA. I-75 exit 16, Georgetown.
    Tours Tuesday and Thursday by reservation. 868-3027.

Headley-Whitney Museum, 4435 Old Frankfort Pike. Open
    April through October, Tuesday through Friday, 10:00
    a.m.-5:00 p.m.; November through March, Wednesday
    through Friday, 10:00 a.m.-5:00 p.m.; weekends,
    noon-5:00 p.m. 255-6653.

Midway Village Guild, P.O. Box 478, Midway, KY 40347.

Midway College. Tours by appointment. 846-4421.

Shakertown at Pleasant Hill, 3500 Lexington Rd.,
    Harrodsburg, KY 40330. 734-5411. Open all year except
    Christmas Eve and Christmas Day.

Harrodsburg Pottery & Crafts, 1026 Lexington Rd. 734-9991.

Old Fort Harrod State Park, US 68 and 127. Most facilities
    are seasonal. Call 1-800-255-PARK.

Beaumont Inn, 638 Beaumont Drive, Harrodsburg KY
    40330. 734-3381. Closed from mid-December to
    mid-March.

Danville-Boyle County Tourist Commission, P.O. Box 1168, Danville, KY 40422. 236-7794.

Centre College, W. Walnut St. For tours call 236-5211.

Constitution Square State Historic Site, 105 E. Walnut St., Danville, KY 40422-1817. 236-5089.

The Elmwood Inn, 205 E. Fourth St., Perryville, KY 40422. Closed Monday. 332-2271.

Perryville Battlefield State Historic Site, Box 296, Perryville, KY 40468. Most facilities are seasonal. 332-8631.

Springfield-Washington County Chamber of Commerce, 208 W. Main St., Springfield, KY 40069. 336-3810.

All numbers are within area code 502.

Lincoln Homestead State Park and Lincoln Boyhood Home: For information, write Hodgenville/LaRue County Chamber of Commerce, P.O. Box 176, Lincoln Square, Hodgenville, KY 42748. Or call 358-3411.

Maker's Mark, Loretto, KY 40037. 865-2099. Open to visitors Monday through Saturday, 10:30 a.m.-3:30 p.m.

Gethsemane Farms Trappist Monastery: For farm products or inquiries on the retreat house, write Gethsemane Farms, Trappist, KY 40051, or call 549-3117.

Bardstown Tourist Commission, Box 867, Bardstown, KY 40004. 1-800-638-4877.

Wickland, one half mile east on US 62. Tours from 9:00 a.m. to sundown; Sunday, noon-sundown.

St. Joseph Proto-Cathedral, 310 W. Stephen Foster Ave. Open Monday through Friday, 9:00 a.m.-5:00 p.m.; Saturday, 9:00 a.m.-3:00 p.m.; Sunday, 1:00-5:00 p.m.

Jailer's Inn, 111 W. Stephen Foster Ave. 348-5551.

Bruntwood Inn Bed & Breakfast, 714 N. Third St. 348-8218.

Kenmore Farms Bed & Breakfast, 1050 Bloomfield Rd.
348-8023.

My Old Kentucky Home State Park, P.O. Box 123,
Bardstown, KY 40004-0323. 348-3502. Nine-hole golf
course, tennis, campsites.

9 ~

Southeast

Kentucky

Take I-64 and I-75 to various routes.

Highlights: *Wonderful parks, small towns, rolling farm country, crafts, coal-mining country, caves, and canyons.*

I shall not leave these prisoning hills
Though they topple their barren heads to level earth
And the forests slide uprooted out of the sky.
Though the waters of Troublesome, of Trace Ford,
Of Sand Lick rise in a single body to glean the valleys,
To drown lush pennyroyal, to unravel rail fences;
Though the sun-ball breaks the ridges into dust
And burns its strength into the blistered rock
I cannot leave. I cannot go away.

—James Still, a poet who lived for many years
in a log house on Dead Mare Branch of Little Carr Creek
in Knott County, Kentucky

Southeast Kentucky is a land of spectacular scenery, hills and hollers, coal mines and the scars left from strip mining, churches, small to tiny towns, and pockets of entrenched poverty, all dominated by the guardian mountains.

The isolation of Appalachia is gradually wearing away, with television and video movie rentals serving as windows on the outside world, but a hardscrabble way of life remains, along with a traditional suspicion of strangers. A touch of mystery, like mist, lingers in the mountain air.

This is an area difficult to fit into any kind of see-the-sights tour. Here, more than anywhere else, you should take a chance, try the unfamiliar road.

Instead of following a tour, choose an appealing state park and use that as a base of operations while exploring the countryside. We suggest five parks, all different, all in beautiful surroundings: Natural Bridge, Buckhorn Lake, Jenny Wiley, Breaks Interstate, and Pine Mountain.

Many famous Kentuckians began life in a log cabin like this one

118

Natural Bridge State Resort Park

From Lexington to the park is a fifty-two-mile drive. Points of interest near the park include Winchester, Mount Sterling, Owingsville, Pilot Knob State Nature Preserve and the Red River Gorge, Beattyville, and Booneville.

From Lexington, take I-64 east to Winchester. Surrounded by rolling farm country, Winchester is the home of Ale-8-One, a popular ginger-flavored soft drink locally produced since 1926 and available only in the area. If you stop in Winchester, it seems a shame not to try a bottle of Ale-8-One. Tours of the bottling plant can be arranged. Get your free samples and visit a unique gift shop.

Suggested side trip: You'll find two nice little towns just east of Winchester. Mount Sterling, established in 1793, is known for its historic Court Day on the third Monday of October. The festivities begin the preceding Saturday when people arrive ready to buy or swap knives, axe handles, guns, hunting dogs, costume jewelry, furniture, whatever.

Owingsville, eight miles east of Mount Sterling and set on a hill, claims to have "the most beautiful Main Street in eastern Kentucky." Even residents of other towns have been known to agree. Handsome old houses are lined up on either side of Main Street like contestants in a beauty pageant.

From Winchester, take the Mountain Parkway south to KY 11 and follow the signs to Natural Bridge. As you drive toward Stanton, the land is open and rural, with mountains rising like blue shadows in the distance.

Before Stanton, you'll reach the Pilot Knob State Nature Preserve outside of Clay City. This lovely wooded area is marked by Pilot Knob, jutting up 730 feet above its

Natural arch carved by erosion at Daniel Boone National Forest

surroundings. It's said that Daniel Boone stood on Pilot Knob for his first view of the bluegrass country. Wildflowers and ferns grow in profusion in the spring.

Natural Bridge State Resort Park, named for an impressive sandstone arch, is located deep in the Daniel Boone National Forest. You'll find a lake with rainbow trout, a chair lift, eighteen miles of hiking trails, a pool, tennis, miniature golf, a lodge, cottages, and camping. A wildflower weekend takes place on the first of May, a Mountain-style Square Dance and Clogging Festival is held in June, and there's a Mushroom Foray in mid-September.

Natural stone arches abound in this area—more than 150 within five miles—and, curiously, the natural bridge near the lodge is neither the oldest, the largest, nor the most accessible of the lot. Still, nobody is likely to complain.

Natural Bridge was first developed as a tourist attraction by the Kentucky Union Railway Company in the late 1880s. By 1900, 25,000 visitors a year were arriving on excursion trains from Louisville and Lexington. When the Kentucky State Park system was founded in 1929, Natural Bridge, donated by the railway company, became one of the four original state parks.

From our hillside cottage, the trail to Natural Bridge led past moss-covered rocks, small waterfalls, and wildflowers scattered among the trees: violets, trillium, wild iris. (It was probably too early for the small yellow lady's slipper, a state endangered species.) The dogwood was just beginning to bloom, and buds were swelling on the mountain laurel.

Past the natural bridge, a trail led to a large rock ledge and a panoramic view. There were names inscribed on the rock, of course. Someone had worked very hard, carving out the following promise: "My love for Mitzi is like this stone—forever."

"What would you guess has happened to Mitzi?" a blonde hiker asked her companion. His answer: "Probably divorced, two kids, and working in a Wal-Mart near Winchester."

We arrived at the lodge for dinner during a heavy rain, followed by a thunderstorm. All the lights blew out. The waitresses did their best, carrying candles and green fluorescent wands that gave off an eerie glow. When we left, the rain was still heavy, thunder was growling in the mountains, and the darkness was total. We had to be guided back to our hillside cottage by a park ranger and, once inside, groped around helplessly for a while.

Lesson learned: Always travel with a flashlight. Springtime weather in the mountains can be very volatile.

By breakfast time the next morning, the rain had stopped. Robins and woodthrush sang in the woods, and ribbons of mist trailed down the mountain ridges.

The Red River Gorge Geological Area is just outside the park, and guests can pick up a driving map at the lodge.

The drive consists of a thirty-six-mile loop on KY 77 and KY 715, going through an old logging railroad tunnel and following the Red River through a rocky landscape that becomes a riot of redbud, mountain laurel, and rhododendron in the spring.

From the park, take KY 11 northwest to Slade; go underneath the Mountain Parkway interchange and, at the junction of KY 11 and KY 15, turn left. Drive north on KY 15 to KY 77 and turn right toward Nada.

Nada, seen in a spring rain, looked like *nada:* trailers, shacks, privies, piles of trash, a few miserable mongrel dogs, the Nada Baptist Mission. But the scene soon improved.

Geologists estimate the Red River Gorge to be millions of years old; it was carved out of solid rock by rains, winds, running water, and earthquakes. Past the Nada Tunnel, you see glistening rocky cliffs, a fast-moving stream, and trees showing a delicate pattern of green, pink, and white.

Hikers, rock climbers, and backpackers see the Red River Gorge at its best. If you're driving through, try to stop for a little while, at least. A trail off KY 715, beginning at the Chimney Top Scenic Drive, leads easily to Princess Arch and Chimney Top Rock.

The Gladie Cabin, a restored log house used by loggers in the early 1900s, serves as a visitors center and is a good place to get information about trails in the Gorge and the Daniel Boone National Forest.

Just before you reach the cabin, you see something unexpected: plowed land and fences. A highway marker explains:

"Sharecropping for wildlife. Once farmers without land traded their labor for a portion of the crop. That's what is happening now in the National Forest. Farmers plant crops on forest land and leave part for wildlife."

Near Parched Corn Creek, another marker discusses the concept of a wilderness: "Where the earth and its community of life are unburdened by man . . . where man himself is a visitor who does not remain." Well, we could take a hint. We completed the loop, came out at Pine Ridge, and took KY 11 south to Beattyville for lunch.

Beattyville, twenty miles south of Natural Bridge and about seventy miles from Lexington, has the air of an isolated mountain town. Surrounded by foothills of the Appalachian Mountains, it's near the meeting of the North, South, and Middle Forks of the Kentucky River. The Kentucky River Overlook, on River Drive, provides a good view.

The Purple Cow restaurant on Main Street serves breakfast, lunch, and dinner in a friendly atmosphere. "I hear all the gossip in the morning from people stopping in for coffee," our waitress said. "Then I'm fixed for the day."

We sat at the counter and listened to the lunchtime regulars talking about the storm the night before, some night fishermen caught out on the river, a local politician. "He's smarter than he lets on," an elderly man remarked dryly and the others seemed to agree.

The waitress contributed a copy of the Beattyville *Chronicle* when she brought the coffee. "Coy Palmer and a whole group of other horse riders headed up the holler for a ride," read one item; "Laura Jane Thorpe stayed all night at her Papa and Granny Deaton's and spent Saturday night with Mamaw Beulah," read another. A recipe for corncob jelly followed.

From Beattyville, take KY 28 south to Booneville and continue south to Buckhorn State Resort Park. Booneville was named for Daniel Boone, who first visited the south Fork River area in 1767 and returned many times to hunt and do surveying work. One survey of land began: "About 200 poles below where there had been a large Indian horse pen, just above a large meadow on the north side of the creek."

Morris Fork Crafts, which carries quilts as well as other handmade articles, is located outside of Booneville on KY 28 heading southeast. The spacious Buckhorn Log Church, made of massive oak logs, is also on KY 28, a little farther on.

Note: Lake Buckhorn State Resort Park is twenty miles or so southeast of Booneville on KY 28.

Buckhorn Lake State Resort Park

Take I-64 east to the Mountain Parkway; exit at Campton. Take KY 15 south to KY 28 west, then KY 1833 to the park. From Lexington the distance to the park is 124 miles. Points of interest near the park include the coal-mining country around Hazard, Quicksand Crafts at Vest, and the Hindman Settlement School at Troublesome Creek.

This park, with its large and shapely mountain lake green with trees to the water's edge, is a haven for boaters and people who like to fish, and its location in the Redbird part of the Daniel Boone National Forest insures peace and quiet.

The facilities include a lodge, cottages, a pool, a marina, a beach, fishing boats for rent, miniature golf, and tennis. A Spring Craft Fair is held early in May.

The trail to Moonshiner's Hollow follows an old logging road and a stream. With an interpretive trail booklet in hand, we identified the white oak, American beech, tulip poplar, and umbrella magnolia trees; listened, as instructed, to "the sounds of the forest changing with the rising of the wind"; and saw, on our own, a cecropia moth lying in a shaft of sunlight and just beginning to spread its wings.

At the lodge for dinner, we sat by a window with a view of the lake and two bird feeders thick with birds. In a moment, dark clouds rolled in, thunder rumbled, and the birds disappeared. Rain beat against the window. Heavy mist obscured the lake. Twenty minutes later, the sky was blue, the lake shining, the grass green. And the birds were back.

From Buckhorn Lake, take KY 28 east to KY 15, heading south to Hazard. This is real coal-mining country: dramatic, harsh, striking. You pass Tattoo Falls, rocky cliffs shiny with black outcroppings of coal, the remains of strip mines, coal trucks lumbering along the road, and, high on a mountain, a tree standing alone, like a sentinel or an Indian scout.

At Hazard, the signs begin: "La Citadelle," followed by a pointing arrow. If you follow the signs, you'll get a quick tour of Hazard as well as a 2.7-mile drive with some corkscrew turns up to the top of a 2,000-foot mountain with great views of the town and the surrounding countryside.

La Citadelle turns out to be a large white motel overlooking Hazard and the land beyond. It features a pool, a restaurant, the Skyline Room, and a bar called La Pub.

Back downtown: Although coal production is down in this area, Hazard looked lively. Ornamental trees lined Main Street, and there was a lot of action around the county courthouse and a restored 1921 hotel, now called The Grand, with a Chinese restaurant. (Don't let anybody tell you that life isn't changing in Appalachia.)

We stopped in a drugstore and asked if there were any working soda fountains in town. No, said the pharmacist, but he had worked for twenty years in a Hazard drugstore that had "a real soda fountain with a marble counter and floor-to-ceiling fitted wood cabinets for the pharmacy, and big old apothecary jars." All gone. The old drugstore is now a sandwich shop. "But I wish I had those apothecary jars."

At the end of Main Street, we found a used-book store, heavily stocked with paperback romance novels. "Romance, romance, romance! Seems like that's all the people want," the proprietor said, petting an overweight basset hound named Sam.

Sam gave us a soulful look and thumped his tail on the floor in greeting. "He's a good dog," the proprietor said. "But he has one bad habit. If I don't get up at 6:00 a.m. to take him out, he gets up on the bed and walks all over me. I tell him, Sam, you gain any more weight, you're goin' to be breaking bones."

Hazard has an annual Black Gold Festival in September that attracts large crowds with parades, arts and crafts, square dancing and clogging, and country music.

From Hazard, take KY 15 west to US 80. Head northeast to KY 160, then north to Vest. L'il Abner and his Dogpatch family and friends would feel right at home around here, with towns like Democrat, Dwarf, Mousie, Pippa Passes, Rowdy, and Viper. Stinking Creek, beginning in the northeast corner of Knott County, flows through to the Cumberland River.

You never know what lies ahead on these mountain roads; you can travel in solitude for miles, then suddenly there are enough coal trucks to cause a traffic jam. We passed one town where the only visible inhabitants were two dogs sunning themselves in the road, one horse, and a man repairing a rusty truck. A desolate trailer down the road displayed a hopeful sign on its roof: "Prom Dresses For Sale."

Three bumper stickers seen on passing cars: One said "Repent." The next said, "Sin is death." The third said, "Good friends, good food, good whiskey."

Vest, at noon, was quiet. Two men sitting on the steps of the general store were whittling. The Quicksand Crafts Center was a shingled building at the top of a slope. We found the manager out mowing the grass. "It was getting so bad, people might think there's nobody here," she said cheerfully.

At Quicksand, skilled weavers make handsome wool rugs, wall hangings, bedspreads, and tablemats in many colors and styles and will take individual orders. An important part of the Center's program is teaching traditional weaving to interested young women in the area.

"I can tell right away who'll make a good weaver—and who won't," the manager told us. "Weaving is like fishing. So nice and relaxin', if you like it. If you don't like it, you can't learn."

In the next room, a young woman was banging away on a loom; she looked unhappy but perhaps it was visitors she didn't like.

Take KY 160 south, crossing US 80, to Hindman, where you'll find the Hindman Settlement School on the forks of Troublesome Creek. This was the nation's first rural settlement school, founded in 1902 to teach young people starved for education. Now that public schools are much better, and school busses make regular runs on improved roads, Hindman's purpose has broadened to include preservation of the mountain heritage. The school provides special services to the public school system, community activities and services, and workshops on Appalachian life and culture. Visitors are offered a twelve-minute video production on the school and its history, a slide show on folk artist Jean Ritchie, who came from nearby Viper, and a tour of the Hindman campus.

Note: From Hindman, it's about thirty miles northeast on US 80 to Prestonburg and Jenny Wiley State Resort Park.

Jenny Wiley State Resort Park

From Lexington it's approximately 115 miles to the park. Take I-64 to Winchester, then follow the Mountain Parkway southeast to Salyersville. Take KY 114 southeast to Prestonburg, and follow signs to the park. Points of interest nearby include

Salyersville, Paintsville, Butcher Hollow, and the grave of Jenny Wiley.

Salyersville, located on the Licking River, is the only town in Kentucky—perhaps the only town in the United States—with an annual genealogy festival.

The festival, called Founder's Day, takes place Labor Day weekend in September. Hundreds of people in Magoffin County come to town to research and talk about their family histories. Leading the way, the Magoffin County Historical Society presents a book on the history of one family every year. In 1978, the festival's first year, the book was on the Adams family, in honor of William Adams, the town's founder. (The town, first known as Adamsville, was later renamed in honor of a local politician, Sam Salyer.)

Not much has changed in Salyersville. The same names that appeared 200 years ago on land grants show up now in the local telephone book: Adams, Arnett, Bailey, Howard, Montgomery, Prater, Salyer, Whitaker, Wireman.

It's a small, close-knit town, "the kind of place where you can make a call, get a wrong number, and talk for ten minutes," a resident said.

Jenny Wiley is one of the state's most popular parks, open year-round, in beautiful mountain land. It offers a lodge, cottages, and camping in season; a lake, with good fishing; boat docks and rental boats; a pool, nature trails, and golf; and a chairlift to the top of Sugar Camp Mountain.

The 180-mile Jenny Wiley Trail, roughly following an old hunting trail used by Indians and early settlers, begins in South Portsmouth in Greenup County and ends at Jenny Wiley park. (The park lodge provides trail information.)

The Jenny Wiley Theater, a major attraction, presents musical comedies, Kentucky Opry shows, and *The Jenny Wiley Story* in an outdoor amphitheater from mid-June through August.

A long list of special events includes an Old Christmas celebration early in January, a St. Patrick's Square Dance, and a Kentucky Highlands Folk Festival in mid-September.

Take US 23 ("the Loretta Lynn highway") north to Butcher Hollow, where country music star Loretta Lynn and her sister, Crystal Gayle, grew up; it's near the tiny town of Van Lear. The tumbledown cabin was rebuilt for *Coal Miner's Daughter*, the movie of Loretta Lynn's life. Continue north on US 23 to Paintsville.

Paintsville was named for Paint Creek, where early settlers found trees stripped of their bark and decorated with drawings of birds and animals painted in red and black. Red and black drawings of buffalo and deer also appeared on the sandstone lining the creek gorge. In time, all the drawings were washed away.

If you toured the impressive Mayo Manor in Ashland, now the Kentucky Highlands Museum (see chapter 5), you may want to see the first Mayo Mansion in Paintsville, built by coal baron John Mayo and his wife Alice in 1912, at Eighth Street and Broadway. (It's now the Our Lady of the Mountains school.) The Mayos both returned to Paintsville in death. Mrs. Mayo is buried behind the mansion; John Mayo's grave is on a hilltop near Paintsville.

There's another grave east of Paintsville, that of Jenny Wiley, a pioneer woman who died in 1831 at the age of seventy-one. (Take KY 40 east to KY 581 and follow signs.)

Jenny Wiley is known for a horrific story of survival that has elements of legend but is supported by historical records. Captured by Shawnees in 1789, she witnessed the slaying of her brother and her five children, was held captive for many months, escaped in this area of Kentucky, and was found by a hunting party of settlers. She was reunited with her husband, Thomas, and had five more children.

Note: From Jenny Wiley State Resort Park, near Prestonsburg, to Breaks Interstate Park is about fifty miles.

Breaks Interstate Park

From Prestonsburg, take US 23 southeast to Pikeville. Continue southeast on US 23/80 to Elkhorn City and follow signs to Breaks Interstate Park. Points of interest near the park include Pikeville, Whitesburg and Appalshop, the Lilley Cornett Woods, and Harlan. The park is about 160 miles from Lexington.

This park, on the Kentucky-Virginia border, is jointly sponsored by the two states. "And if you think that's confusing, try dealing with three phone systems, the way we do," said a clerk at the lodge. (We'd already noticed that getting a call through can be tricky.)

The road from Prestonsburg is, briefly, one shopping mall after another. Then it's an up-and-down road following Greasy Creek.

Pikeville was the center of the famous Hatfield-McCoy feud, which began during the Civil War and raged until the 1890s. Randolph McCoy, a leader of his clan, is buried in Dils cemetery on the outskirts of town.

The amazing "Pikeville Cut-Thru," on new US 23, shows what happens when a town decides to move a mountain, a river, a railroad, and a major highway.

Many mountain people are touchy about the term "hillbilly," but not, apparently, in Pikeville, where they have a weekend Hillbilly Days Festival in early April.

Obituary taken from an 1888 Pikeville newspaper: " 'Bucktooth John' Collins departed this vale of tears in the year of our Lord 1879. His demise was caused by his having accused 'Bad Andy' Sizemore of stealing a hog."

Breaks Interstate Park contains 4,600 acres of rugged, wonderful country and the Breaks, the largest canyon east of the Mississippi, carved by the Russell Fork River. The canyon is a magnificent sight—a five-mile cut with the river foaming between 1,000-foot palisades. The countryside is a deep green in the summer, a mass of flowers in the spring when the rhododendron bloom, and a brilliant show of red and gold in the fall.

The park maintains a lodge, open from spring through the fall. Cottages are available year-round, campsites in season. The Visitor's Center has coal-mining exhibits as well as maps and information. There's a pool, hiking trails, white-water rafting, fishing in Laurel Lake, caves, and hidden springs. Among other events on the park calendar are square dancing and bluegrass music in July, a Gospel Song Festival on Labor Day weekend, and white-water rafting for novices and experts on the Russell Fork of the Big Sandy in October.

From our room we had a view of the gorge, breathtaking in the sunset, and the unceasing sound of wind and rushing water to sing us to sleep.

Before dinner, we took a walk and saw the view from Pinnacle Rock and several other overlooks. I found myself remembering what a friend had said about the Grand Canyon: "It's overwhelming . . . after a while, you're worn out and can't *look* anymore."

At dinner in the Rhododendron Lodge, we talked to the waitress about the Breaks. "I've lived here all my life, so I sort of take it for granted," she said. "When we were kids, we'd climb the cliffs, shoot down the river. Mercy! We must have had guardian angels."

The history of the Breaks is full of tall tales: of feuds, hidden fortunes in silver and pirate gold, Indian caves, and bootleggers' hideouts.

Back at the lodge for breakfast, our attention was directed to the Towers, a castellated sandstone formation rising 1,600 feet into two wooded pinnacles. An American flag hung from a top tree branch on the left Tower. "How *did* the flag get there?" we asked, looking through binoculars at the churning river water and the steep cliffs below the tree line.

Then we heard the story. The first flag was planted on the Tower by a local boy, a reckless teenager who was killed in a motorcycle accident a year or so later. By then, the flag had disappeared; winds are fierce in the Breaks. His friends managed to hang another flag as a memorial. In time, that, too, disappeared. The third flag appeared at the time of the Gulf War. "Crazy kids," said the breakfast waitress, sounding unsympathetic. "I'd want a better reason to risk my neck."

Leaving Breaks Park and Elkhorn City, take US 119 west to Whitesburg. You see hills, streams, flowering trees, butterflies, signs pointing the way to towns like Lookout and Neon, and roadside flea markets. One displayed for-sale items on the hoods of several battered cars.

Some little towns look half-empty. "People with any get up and go," it's said, "have got up and went."

On the other hand, you see "tanning salons" in villages that aren't much more than a gas station and a general store. Glimpses of cabins and trailers half-hidden in the hills suggest how much of mountain life is out of sight. There are stories of snake-handling religious cults. Of heavy betting on illegal "chicken fights." Of marijuana replacing bootleg whiskey as the cash crop. "The big shopping day in town used to be when people got their welfare checks. Now it's when the marijuana crop comes in."

Sheltered by the surrounding mountains, Whitesburg is the home of Appalshop, a remarkable non-profit arts and education center devoted to the culture and concerns of the people of Appalachia. "Stop by, you'll enjoy it," a bearded man told us when we asked directions. "I hang out there all the time."

Appalshop hums with activity, producing documentaries, records, concerts, exhibits, and readings. June Appal Recordings, Roadside Theater, Headwaters Television, and the community radio station, WMMT-FM, are all offshoots of the center. An important yearly festival of traditional mountain arts, "Seedtime on the Cumberland," is held at Appalshop during the first weekend in June.

Visitors are welcome. There's usually an art or photography exhibit, and a splendid quilt is on permanent (I hope) display at the head of the stairs. You can ask for a tour or a screening of one of Appalshop's documentary videos: *On Our Own Land,* for instance, or *Quilting Women.*

On Our Own Land deals with a long battle to reform the broad-form deed, a 1908 statute allowing companies that owned mineral rights to mine the land by any method they chose, with little or no payment to the owner. An amendment passed in 1988 gave more protection to the rights of Kentucky landowners.

Whitesburg is also the home of Franklin Gary Powers, the U-2 pilot shot down over Russia during the Eisenhower administration—something we learned while walking down Main Street toward the Courthouse Café.

"Pilot . . . Spy . . . Hero," reads the historical marker on Main Street, adding that the "U-2 incident catapulted certain activities of the United States into world view." Powers was tried and imprisoned in Russia, swapped for a Russian spy, and returned to the United States. Did he come back to Whitesburg? The marker says only that he died some years later in a civilian helicopter crash.

The Courthouse Café is a bright and busy place, with quilts and local art work displayed on brick walls, and a good lunchtime selection of soups, salads, and sandwiches.

If possible, take time to see the Lilley Cornett Woods, 554 acres of old-growth forest and a rare chance to see what much of Kentucky looked like before the logging industry swept through.

From Whitesburg, take KY 160 north to KY 588 and follow signs. Take a picnic lunch along, and a can of bug spray. To protect the woods, only guided tours are allowed, but the guides, helpful and informative, are an added asset.

Return to US 119 via KY 7 west. Take KY 699 south to Leatherwood and KY 221 south to US 119. (The detour may sound longer than it is; the extra distance is nineteen miles.)

Harlan is an atmospheric old mining town, hidden away in a valley between Big and Little Black mountains. The summit of Black Mountain, at 4,145 feet, is the highest point in Kentucky.

First called Mount Pleasant, the town was renamed to honor Major Silas Harlan, killed at the Battle of Blue Licks in 1782. Its history is darkened by bitter and violent strikes in the coal mines; the last was the subject of a prize-winning documentary, *Harlan County, U.S.A.*

Harlan today is peaceful in its mountain setting. In the courthouse square you'll notice war memorials, a couple of cannons, a historical marker listing the twenty-two courthouses burned during the Civil War, and another on Major Silas Harlan. The old men who sit on the benches before the courthouse seem rooted to the spot. Wearing overalls and high-topped shoes, they whittle, chew tobacco, and watch the passing parade.

The lunch counter at Creek's Drugstore, on Central Street near the courthouse, is a local gathering place. "And Violet, the cashier, she's great," a Harlan resident said. "Only woman I know who laughs with a hillbilly accent."

Harlan has a Poke Sallit Festival the last weekend in June, with string bands, a man cooking pork rind cracklings in the courthouse yard, cornhusk flowers and dolls for sale, and

T-shirts spray-painted on the spot. (Shirts emblazoned with "My Achy Breaky Heart" were the big seller last year.)

Jay's Sandwich Shop, on Main Street, serves poke sallit along with a traditional plate of ham, green onions, corn-bread, and a glass of buttermilk.

Poke sallit is made of the young leaves of the wild poke plant when it first appears in the spring. Bessie Bolt, in *The Foxfire Book of Appalachian Cookery*, writes: "My mother told me that an old doctor said if you eat three messes of poke in the spring it would doctor you free of any fevers. . . . The way I cook poke is I boil it, squeeze it out, and put oil on it." She also added a diced cooked onion; other cooks like slices of hard-boiled egg, or a little sowbelly in the cooking water.

From Harlan, take US 119 southwest to Pine Mountain.

Pine Mountain State Resort Park

You'll find Pine Mountain approximately 114 miles from Lexington. Take I-75 south to Corbin and US 25E southeast to the park. Points of interest include the Cumberland Gap National Historic Park and Corbin.

This lovely mountain hideaway became Kentucky's first state park in 1926. After the Laurel Cove amphitheater was built in a natural forest cove, the first Mountain Laurel Festival was held in 1935. It's still a big event in Pineville when the laurel is in full bloom, the last weekend in May, and the whole town turns out for the gala parade.

The Great American Dulcimer Convention, another outside event, is held in late September.

Pine Mountain's Nature Preserve is a special place, a stately old-growth forest with rare wildflowers and birds as well as ancient trees.

Pine Mountain Park has a lodge, cottages, camping, nine miles of hiking trails, a pool, and golf.

We had an attractive cottage with a fireplace and a blooming dogwood tree by the front door. The well-equipped kitchen inspired an immediate trip to Pineville for supplies. The store had plenty of Moon Pies, sliced white bread in packages large enough to feed an orphanage, and, at the deli counter, three kinds of jello salad, pickled eggs, ham, chitlins, and pickled pigs' feet. "We eat everything but the squeal," mountain people say about pigs.

You'll find several craft centers near Pineville: Henderson Settlement and Laurel Fork Crafts and Kathy's Needle and Thread (weaving, hand-quilting, and tacking), both eighteen miles southwest of Pineville on KY 190, and Red Bird Mission Crafts (hickory bark furniture, baskets, pottery, and hand-woven rugs), twenty-eight miles north on KY 66.

From Pineville, take US 25E south past Middleboro to Cumberland Gap National Historic Park.

The Cumberland Gap, a deep natural break in the Cumberland Mountains, served as a pioneer gateway to the West and is one of the most famous mountain passes in the United States. A trail leading westward was known to the Shawnees as *Athawominee* (the Warrior's Path). Daniel Boone and thirty "axe men" followed this trail in 1775 as they cut a new trail to Fort Boonesborough. This became known as Boone's Trace, or the Wilderness Road.

The legendary Daniel Boone has obscured the man, a scout who said, in his old age, that he was never lost in the wilderness but could recall being "bewildered for about three days." He was not illiterate; on occasion, he took a copy of *Gulliver's Travels* to read on surveying trips. He never wore a coonskin cap. His oldest son was captured and killed by Indians; another son died at the Battle of Blue Licks. Boone himself was captured by the Shawnees and was a veteran of many Indian attacks. Still, he never became an Indian hater. He called the Shawnee chief Blackfish "one of Nature's noblemen" and said that he was sorry to have killed any Indians "for they have always been kinder to me than the whites."

By the end of the Revolutionary War in 1783, nearly 10,000 settlers had come through the Cumberland Gap, following Boone's trail. By 1800, the number was more than 200,000. The vast herds of buffalo that had roamed Kentucky were gone. Towns were springing up. Land speculators were busy. The race was on.

The view from Pinnacle Mountain is a marvel on a clear day, and just as impressive on a day of mist and fog, with thunder speaking of a coming storm. In any weather, you're likely to see the shadows of the first scouts—Thomas Walker in 1750, Colonel James Smith in 1766, Daniel Boone and John Findlay's first exploration in 1769—and the settlers who followed those first trails with hope, like a strong wind, driving them on.

The Cumberland Gap National Historical Park covers 20,000 acres and the crest of the Cumberland Mountains where Kentucky, Virginia, and Tennessee meet. There are fifty miles of trails, two caves, and Civil War fortifications around the Gap area. The Ridge Trail on Brush Mountain leads to the Hensley Settlement, a restored 1903 mountain community.

Take US 25E north to Pineville and continue to Corbin and I-75. A large billboard just outside of Corbin says, "Eat where it all began—Colonel Sanders Fried Chicken—ask anyone."

We asked an elderly man in downtown Corbin. He gave us directions and then hesitated, as if he knew a joke he had just decided not to tell us (a feeling we often had in similar small-town conversations). "Tell you this: Sanders's place looks a lot better now than it did then," he finally said, and walked on.

The Harlan Sanders Café, with flowers and shrubs at the entrance, looks bright and brand new, in spite of being on the National Register of Historic Places.

Sanders moved to Corbin in 1930 and opened a gas station and, behind it, a lunchroom so small that only six people could be seated. By 1937, the place had expanded to seat 142 and fried chicken was the popular choice on the menu. After a fire in 1939, Sanders reopened the business as a restaurant and motel, Sanders Court & Café, which did well until the construction of I-75 bypassed Corbin.

"Birth of a legend," begins a plaque just outside the café, "Kentucky's most famous citizen." (Move aside, Daniel Boone and Abraham Lincoln.) "Born on Sept. 9, 1890, he left home at 12 to support his family . . . jobs as farmhand, soldier, railroader, secretary, insurance salesman and ferryboat operator . . . came to Corbin in 1930. . . . During the Depression, he began selling food to tourists. His food was liked. In 1932, he bought a small restaurant near this site. . . . Here he created, developed, and perfected his world-famous Kentucky Fried Chicken recipe."

The plaque concludes: "Presented by the innumerable friends of Kentucky's greatest goodwill ambassador."

The exhibits inside are both interesting and evocative. You'll find replicas of Sanders's office and kitchen, a 1940 pressure cooker used for cooking chicken, a model motel room, an old newspaper ad ("H. Sanders Court & Café. Corbin's First & Finest. Known from Canada to Cuba. 32 rooms— 32 baths"), handwritten recipe for Swiss steak, a motel room bill, dated 1956, for $4.00, a scroll naming Harlan Sanders an honorary Kentucky colonel. Afterward, you can walk into a gleaming Kentucky Fried Chicken restaurant and have lunch.

Frontier scouts, opening up the Cumberland Gap, set the stage for irrevocable change. Harlan Sanders, frying chicken in Corbin, Kentucky, was another front-runner—a symbol of the coming fast-food revolution that would alter the look and customs of the country.

In the Area

Winchester Tourist Information Center, 2 S. Maple St., Suite A, Winchester, KY 40391. 606-744-0556.

Ale-8-One Bottling Co., 25 Carol Rd. 606-744-3484. Gift shop open Monday through Friday, 8:30 a.m.-4:30 p.m. Tours by appointment. Best days to visit, Monday and Thursday.

Pilot Knob State Nature Preserve, Clay City. 502-564-2886.

Natural Bridge State Resort Park, General Delivery, Slade, KY 40376-9999. 606-663-2214 or 1-800-325-1710.

Lee County Tourism, 219 Radio Station Loop, Beattyville, KY 41311. 606-464-3600.

Morris Fork Crafts, 930 Morris Fork Rd., Booneville, KY 606-398-2194.

Buckhorn Log Church. Tours 9:00 a.m.-5:00 p.m. daily. 606-398-7245.

Buckhorn Lake State Resort Park, HC 36, Box 1000, Buckhorn, KY 41721-9602. 606-398-7510 or 1-800-325-0058.

Perry County Tourism, Hazard, KY 41701. 606-439-2659.

La Citadelle, 651 Skyline Drive, Hazard. 606-436-2126.

Quicksand Craft Center, KY 160, Vest. Monday through Friday, 8:00 a.m.-5:00 p.m.

Hindman Settlement School, 17 miles northeast of Hazard, KY 80 to KY 160. Monday through Friday, 9:00 a.m.-5:00 p.m. 606-785-5475.

Jenny Wiley State Resort Park, HC 66, Box 200, Prestonsburg, KY 41654-9799. 606-886-2711 or 1-800-325-9799.

Paintsville Tourist Commission, P.O. Box 71, Paintsville, KY 41240. 1-800-542-5790.

Mayo Mansion, Eighth and Broadway. Tours by appointment. 606-789-5688.

Pikeville-Pike County Tourism Commission, P.O. Box 149, Pikeville, KY 41502. 1-800-844-7453.

Breaks Interstate Park, P.O. Box 100, Breaks, VA 24607. 703-865-4413. For motel reservations: Breaks Motor Lodge, P.O. Box 99, Breaks, VA 24607. 703-865-4414.

Whitesburg Tourist Commission, P.O. Box 520, Whitesburg, KY 41858. 606-633-8034.

Appalshop, 306 Madison St., Whitesburg, KY 41858. 606-633-0108.

Lilley Cornett Woods. For information: Supt., HC 63, Box 2710, Skyline, KY 41851. 606-633-5828. Guided tours, April through October by appointment.

Pine Mountain State Resort Park, 1050 State Park Road, Pineville, KY 40977-0610. 606-337-3066 or 1-800-325-1712.

Henderson Settlement and Laurel Fork Crafts, KY 190, 18 miles southwest of Pineville. Monday through Friday, 8:00 a.m.-4:30 p.m. 606-337-5823.

Kathy's Needle and Thread, Route 2, Box 118, Pineville, KY 40977. 606-337-6753.

Red Bird Mission Crafts, 26 miles north of Pineville on KY 66, Beverly, KY. Monday through Saturday. 606-598-2709.

City of Corbin, Tourist & Convention Commission, 101 N. Lynn Ave. 606-528-6390.

Harlan Sanders Café & Museum. Open daily, 7:00 a.m.-11:00 p.m. I-75, exit 29, south on US 25E one mile, right on US 25W.

Epilogue:
One Last Look

One particular scene seems to sum up the appeal of travel in Kentucky, the beauty of the countryside, the historical background, the chance meetings with memorable people.

We had spent the night in Shakertown at Pleasant Hill and in the morning, it was time to leave. But first we drove to the West Lot, a part of Shakertown we hadn't seen before, past stone fences, ducks in a pond, rolling farmland, woods, the water of Shawnee Run Creek shimmering in the sunlight. A woman was comfortably seated under a tree near the water—sketching, we thought—and a man seemed to be sitting in the middle of the creek. Oh well, we thought, and went on.

It was a brilliant day in late September, the leaves just beginning to turn, and the buildings in the West Lot—a large farmhouse, a stone wash house, black barns, a large red barn, green fields marked off by stone fences—stood sharp-edged against a bright blue sky. We were alone there. Black-eyed Susans still bloomed by the house steps and a cardinal sang somewhere in the trees. Slavery, war, hard times—all had come and gone. The Shakers had failed in their effort to create a small and better world. Their buildings and the pastoral land remained. It was a scene that still seemed to promise something.

On our way back, we stopped by the creek and spoke to the woman sitting on the grass. I forget why; we wanted to know the time, the right route to Frankfort, something. An easy and delightful conversation developed. Her husband, it

141

turned out, *was* sitting in the middle of the creek on a small camp stool. "It's something he likes to do," she explained. "So peaceful." She had a pad of paper in her lap and was not sketching, but writing notes for a Ph.D. dissertation on teaching philosophy to fifth-grade students. She asked about our visit and we talked about Kentucky awhile.

"My family came to Kentucky in 1790," she said. "I like living here. One reason is that Kentuckians are all eccentrics. At least," she added proudly, "everybody *I* know is. It makes life interesting. You just never know what to expect."

Index

AMUSEMENT PARKS
  Guntown Mountain, Cave
    City, 71
  Kentucky Action Park, Cave
    City, 71
ANTIQUES, CRAFTS and
  GIFT SHOPS
  Antique malls, Cadiz, 63, 64
  Ashland Area Art Gallery &
    Artists' Market, Ashland,
    58
  Bailey's Country Store,
    Williamsburg, 91
  Bardstown Road, Louisville,
    14
  Boone Tavern Gift Shop,
    Berea, 86
  Broadbent's Food & Gifts,
    Cadiz, 63
  Bybee Pottery, Richmond, 85
  Crackerbarrel, Richmond, 85
  Doe Run Inn, Brandenburg,
    20
  Eleanor Beard Studio,
    Hardinsburg, 21
  Frankfort Avenue,
    Louisville, 14
  Galante Studio,
    Hardinsburg, 21
  Harrodsburg Pottery and
    Crafts, Harrodsburg, 103
  Hazel Antique Mall, Hazel,
    34

Henderson Settlement and
  Laurel Fork Crafts,
  Pineville, 136
Holbrook Drugstore,
  Morehead, 58–59
Indian Gift Shop, Cave City,
  71
Irish Acres Antiques,
  Ashland, 58
Joe Ley Antiques, Louisville,
  13–14
Kathy's Needle and Thread,
  Pineville, 136
Lancaster Antique Market,
  Lancaster, 87
A Likely Story, Maysville,
  49
Loch Lea Antiques, Paris, 96
Moberly Grocery,
  Richmond, 85
Morris Fork Crafts,
  Booneville, 124
Piedmont Gallery, Augusta,
  46
Quicksand Crafts Center,
  Vest, 126–127
Rags 'n Nags, Lexington, 97
Railroad Street, Midway,
  82–83
Red Bird Mission Crafts,
  Pineville, 136
Russellville, 68
Toll Gate Shop, Loretto, 110

ANTIQUES, CRAFTS and
GIFT SHOPS (*cont.*)
Washington, 51
Wickliffe Mounds museum,
Wickliffe, 31

BAKERIES, BOTTLING
PLANTS and
DISTILLERIES
Ale-8-One, Winchester, 119
Burk's Mill and Distillery,
Loretto, 108–110
Elijah Craig bourbon,
Bardstown, 99
Schlabach's Bakery, Elkton, 68
BOATING and FISHING
Ballard County Wildlife
Management Area, Oscar,
30
Belle of Louisville, Louisville,
11, 16
Big South Fork National
River and Recreation Area,
Blue Heron, 89–90
Breaks Interstate Park,
Breaks, 130–132
Buckhorn Lake State Resort
Park, Buckhorn, 124–125
Carter Caves State Resort
Park, Olive Hill, 52–53
Cumberland Falls State
Resort Park, Corbin, 88–89
Daniel Boone National
Forest, Morehead, 59
Dixie Belle, Pleasant Hill, 102
Greenbo Lake State Park,
Greenup, 54–55
Jenny Wiley State Resort
Park, Prestonsburg, 128

John James Audubon State
Park, Henderson, 23
Jubilee 1, Paducah, 26
Kentucky Dam Village State
Resort Park, Gilbertsville,
36
Lake Barkley State Resort
Park, Cadiz, 63
Land Between the Lakes,
40–41, 41
Miss Green River II, Cave
City, 73
Natural Bridge State Resort
Park, Slade, 120–122
Paint Lick, 4
Poppin Rock Boat Ramp,
Morehead, 59
BOTTLING PLANTS. See
BAKERIES, BOTTLING
PLANTS and
DISTILLERIES
BRIDGES and FERRIES
Augusta to Boude's Landing,
46
Bennett's Mill bridge, 55
Cabin Creek Bridge, 52
Dover Bridge, 51–52
Goddard White Bridge, 60
Lincoln Trail Bridge,
Hawesville, 22
Marion to Cave-in-Rock, 24
Oldtown bridge, 55
Sand Lick Creek bridge, 60
Simon Kenton Bridge,
Maysville to Aberdeen,
47
Suspension bridge,
Covington, 1
Valley Pike Bridge, 51
Wickliffe to Cairo, 31

Index

CAVES and NATURAL SITES
  The Barrens, 63
  The Breaks, Breaks, 130–131
  Carter Caves State Resort
    Park, Olive Hill, 53
  Cascade Cave, Olive Hill, 53
  Crystal Cave, Cave City, 73
  Cumberland Gap, 136, 137
  Hidden River Cave, Horse
    Cave, 74–76
  The Knobs, 63
  Mammoth Cave National
    Park, Cave City, 73–74
  Mississippi Flyway, 30–31
  Monkey's Eyebrow,
    Bandana, 29–30
  Moonbows, Corbin, 88, 89
  New Madrid fault, Hickman,
    33–34
  Onyx Cave, Cave City, 71
  Pennyroyal, 62–63
  Red River Gorge Geological
    Area, Nada, 122–123
  Stone arches, Slade, 121
  The Towers, Breaks, 131–132
CEMETERIES. See WAR SITES
  and CEMETERIES
CHURCHES, MONASTERIES,
  RETREATS and SHRINES
  Buckhorn Log Church,
    Booneville, 124
  Cane Ridge Shrine, Paris,
    97
  Gethsemane Farms Trappist
    Monastery, Gethsemane,
    110–111, 111
  Indian Creek Baptist
    Church, Cynthiana, 95–96
  St. Joseph's Cathedral,
    Bardstown, 112

CITIES and TOWNS
  Adamsville. See Salyersville
  Ashland, 56–58
  Augusta, 45–47
  Bardstown, 111–113
  Beattyville, 123
  Berea, 85–87
  Big Boiling Springs. See
    Russellville
  Booneville, 123–124
  Bowling Green, 70–71
  Brandenburg, 20–21
  Butcher Hollow, 129
  Cadiz, 63
  Carlisle, 95
  Carrollton, 5–7
  Cave City, 71–74
  Caverna. See Horse Cave
  Cayce, 33
  Cloverport, 22
  Columbus, 32
  Corbin, 87–88, 137–138
  Covington, 1
  Danville, 105
  Dawson Springs, 37, 39
  Elkton, 67–68
  Energy. See Land Between
    the Lakes
  Fenton. See Land Between
    the Lakes
  Fort Knox, 19–20
  Georgetown, 83, 98–99
  Germantown, 47
  Gethsemane, 110–111
  Ghent, 4–5
  Golden Pond, 39–40
  Greenup, 53–56
  Hardinsburg, 21
  Harlan, 134–135
  Harrodsburg, 103–104

CITIES and TOWNS (*cont.*)
Hawesville, 22
Hazard, 125–126
Hazel, 34–35
Hematite. See Land Between
   the Lakes
Henderson, 23–24
Hickman, 33
Hindman, 127
Hopewell. See Paris
Hopkinsville, 64–66
Horse Cave, 74–76
Lancaster, 87
Land Between the Lakes,
   39–42
Limestone Landing. See
   Maysville
Loretto, 108–110
Louisville, 9–16
Marion, 24
Mattoon, 24
Mayfield, 35–36
Maysville, 47–51, 92–93
McCool's Creek. See Ghent
Midway, 82–83, 99–100
Milton, 7
Morehead, 58–59
Mount Pleasant. See
   Harlan
Mount Sterling, 119
Murray, 34
Nada, 122
New Madrid Bend, 33–34
Oscar, 30–31
Owensboro, 22–23
Owingsville, 119
Paducah, 24–26
Paintsville, 129
Paris, 96–97
Perryville, 105–106
Pikeville, 130

Poage Settlement. See
   Ashland
Princeton, 37–38
Rabbit Hash, 2–4
Richmond, 85
Rock Haven, 20
Russellville, 68
Salyersville, 128
South Union, 68–70
Springfield, 107
Vanceburg, 52
Vest, 126–127
Warsaw, 4
Washington, 47, 50–51, 92–93
Whitesburg, 132–133
W-Hollow, 54, 55
Wickliffe, 31
Williamsburg, 90–91
Winchester, 119
COLLEGES, SCHOOLS and
   UNIVERSITIES
Appalshop, Whitesburg,
   132–133
Berea College, Berea, 86
Centre College, Danville, 105
Cumberland College,
   Williamsburg, 90
Eastern Kentucky
   University, Richmond, 85
Georgetown College,
   Georgetown, 98
Hindman Settlement School,
   Hindman, 127
Hopkinsville Community
   College, Hopkinsville, 64
Midway College, Midway,
   100
Morehead State University,
   Morehead, 58
Murray State University,
   Murray, 34

Western Kentucky
University, Bowling
Green, 70
CRAFTS. See ANTIQUES,
CRAFTS and GIFT SHOPS
CREEKS, LAKES, RIVERS and
SPRINGS
Big Sandy River, 44
Carter Run Lake, 59
Cumberland River, 40
Doe Run Creek, 20
Greenbo Lake, 54
Green River, 73
Kentucky Lake, 40
Lake Barkley, 40, 63
Mississippi River, 44
Ohio River, 19–26, 44
Otter Creek, 20
Royal Spring, Georgetown,
98
Sinking Spring,
Hodgenville, 107
Smokey Valley Lake, 52
Tennessee River, 40
Tennessee Valley Authority,
40–42
Tug Fork River, 44
Wolf Creek, 21

DEPOSITORIES. See
LIBRARIES and
DEPOSITORIES
DISTILLERIES. See
BAKERIES, BOTTLING
PLANTS and
DISTILLERIES

FERRIES. See BRIDGES and
FERRIES

FESTIVALS. See SPECIAL
EVENTS
FISHING. See BOATING and
FISHING

GALLERIES, MUSEUMS and
PLANETARIUMS
American Museum of Caves
and Karstlands, Horse
Cave, 75–76
Appalachian Museum,
Berea, 86
Ashland Area Art Gallery &
Artists' Market, Ashland,
58
Blue Licks Battlefield
museum, Blue Licks, 94
Columbus-Belmont
Battlefield State Park
museum, Columbus, 32
Filson Club, Louisville, 12
Fort Boonesborough
museum, Richmond, 83
General William Clark
Market House Museum,
Paducah, 26
Golden Pond Visitor Center,
Land Between the Lakes,
41–42
Harlan Sanders Cafe &
Museum, Corbin, 87–88,
137–138
Headley-Whitney Museum,
Midway, 99
International Museum of the
Horse, Lexington, 81–82
J.B. Speed Museum,
Louisville, 11
John James Audubon
Museum, Henderson, 23

GALLERIES, MUSEUMS and
PLANETARIUMS (*cont.*)
Kentucky Art and Crafts
Gallery, Louisville, 13
Kentucky Highlands
Museum, Ashland, 56–58,
129
Kentucky Museum and
Library, Bowling Green,
71
Lancaster historical
museum, Lancaster, 87
Mason County Museum,
Maysville, 49
Mining museum, Blue
Heron, 90
MSU Folk Art Gallery,
Morehead, 58
Museum of History and
Science, Louisville, 13
Museum of the American
Quilter's Society,
Paducah, 25–26
National Corvette Museum,
Bowling Green, 71
National Scouting Museum,
Murray, 34
Northeastern Kentucky
History Museum, Olive
Hill, 53
Old Bardstown Village and
Civil War Museum,
Bardstown, 112
Old Church Museum,
Washington, 50
Patton Museum of Cavalry
and Armor, Fort Knox, 19
Pennyroyal Area Museum,
Hopkinsville, 65
Perryville Battlefield
museum, Perryville, 106

Wickliffe Mounds museum,
Wickliffe, 31
GIFT SHOPS. See ANTIQUES,
CRAFTS and GIFT SHOPS

HISTORIC BUILDINGS
Buckner Homestead,
Brandenburg, 21
Butler-Turpin House,
Carrollton, 5–6
Centre House, South Union,
69–70, 101
Conrad-Caldwell House,
Louisville, 12–13
Crockett's Restaurant,
Hopkinsville, 64
Doe Run Inn, Brandenburg,
20
Duncan Tavern, Paris, 96
Federal Hill, Bardstown,
112–113
Forest Retreat Farm, Carlisle,
95
Harrison County
Courthouse, Cynthiana, 96
Jefferson County
Courthouse, Louisville, 13
Masterson House,
Carrollton, 6
Mayo Mansion, Paintsville,
129
McDowell House and
Apothecary Shop,
Danville, 105
Squire Pate House,
Hawesville, 22
Wickland, Bardstown, 112
HISTORIC DISTRICTS
Ashland, 56
Augusta, 46

Bowling Green, 71
Carrollton, 6
Cherokee Triangle,
Louisville, 15
Maysville, 47–49
Old Louisville, 12–13
Russellville, 68
Washington, 50
HISTORIC SITES and
STATUES
Abraham Lincoln Birthplace
National Historic Site,
Hodgenville, 107, 108
Buffalo Furnace, Greenup,
55
Carry A. Nation Birthplace,
Lancaster, 87
Chief Fly Smith,
Hopkinsville, 65–66
Chief Paduke, Paducah, 26
Chief Whitepath,
Hopkinsville, 65–66
Clinton Furnace, Ashland, 56
Constitution Square State
Historic Site, Danville, 105
Daniel Boone, Louisville, 15
Dinsmore Homestead,
Burlington, 79–80
General George Rogers
Clark, Louisville, 11
Jefferson Davis Monument,
Fairview, 66–67
Lincoln's Boyhood Home,
Knob Creek, 107–108
Maker's Mark, Loretto,
108–110
Perryville Battlefield State
Historic Site, Perryville,
105–106
Simon Kenton Historic Site,
Washington, 50

Union soldiers monument,
Vanceburg, 52
White Hall State Historic
Site, Richmond, 84
Wooldridge Monuments,
Mayfield, 35–36
HORSES, HORSES, HORSES
Claiborne Farms, Paris, 97
Keeneland Race Course,
Keeneland, 82, 97
Kentucky Horse Park,
Lexington, 81–82, 97
Stone Farm, Paris, 97

INDIAN SITES. See NATIVE
AMERICANS and
INDIAN SITES
INFORMATION CENTERS.
See TOURISM and
INFORMATION
CENTERS
INNS and LODGING
Beaumont Inn,
Harrodsburg, 104
Boone Tavern Hotel, Berea,
86
Breckinridge House,
Georgetown, 83
Brown Hotel, Louisville, 11
Bruntwood Inn Bed and
Breakfast, Bardstown, 112
Carrollton Inn, Carrollton, 6
Doe Run Inn, Brandenburg,
20
Drawbridge Inn, Florence, 2
Elmwood Inn, Perryville, 105
Ghent House Bed &
Breakfast Inn, Ghent, 5
The Grand, Hazard, 125
Jailer's Inn, Bardstown, 112

INNS and LODGING (*cont.*)
  Kenmore Farms, Bardstown,
    112
  La Citadelle, Hazard, 125
  Lamplighter Inn, Augusta,
    46
  Old Louisville Inn Bed &
    Breakfast, Louisville, 12
  Seelbach Hotel, Louisville,
    11–12
  Shaker Tavern, South Union,
    70
  Shakertown, Pleasant Hill,
    102
  Wigwam Village, Cave City,
    71
IN the AREA
  Buffalo Trace, 113–116
  Fort Knox to Paducah, 27–28
  Louisville, 17–18
  North-central Kentucky,
    7–8, 60–61
  South-central Kentucky,
    76–77
  Southeast Kentucky,
    139–140
  Southwest Kentucky, 42–43

LAKES. See CREEKS, LAKES,
  RIVERS and SPRINGS
LIBRARIES and
  DEPOSITORIES
  Gold Depository, Fort Knox,
    19–20
  Jesse Stuart Library and
    Reading Room, Greenup,
    54
LIVING HISTORY SITES
  Adsmore House, Princeton,
    37–38

Fort Boonesborough State
  Park, Richmond, 83–84
Homeplace 1850, Land
  Between the Lakes, 42
Pioneer Weapons Hunting
  Area, Morehead, 59
Shakertown, Pleasant Hill,
  100–103
LODGING. See INNS and
  LODGING

MONASTERIES. See
  CHURCHES,
  MONASTERIES,
  RETREATS and SHRINES
MUSEUMS. See GALLERIES,
  MUSEUMS and
  PLANETARIUMS

NATIONAL REGISTER of
  HISTORIC PLACES
  Bowling Green, 71
  Courthouse square, Carlisle,
    95
  Crockett's Restaurant,
    Hopkinsville, 64
  Harlan Sanders Cafe,
    Corbin, 137
  Rabbit Hash, 2–4
NATIVE AMERICANS and
  INDIAN SITES
  Blue Jacket, 49
  Burial mounds, Bayou du
    Chien, 33
  Central Park mounds,
    Ashland, 58
  Chief Paduke, 26
  Eagle Falls, Corbin, 89
  Mingo Indians, 51

Mound Builders, 31
Shawnee Indians, 51, 55, 59, 83, 129, 136–137
Trail of Tears, Hopkinsville, 65–66
NATURAL SITES. See CAVES and NATURAL SITES

OUTDOOR RECREATION
Ballard County Wildlife Management Area, Oscar, 30
Big South Fork National River and Recreation Area, Blue Heron, 89–90
Blue Licks Battlefield State Park, Blue Licks, 94–95
Braille Trail, Louisville, 15
Breaks Interstate Park, Breaks, Virginia, 130–132
Buckhorn Lake State Resort Park, Buckhorn, 124–125
Carter Caves State Resort Park, Olive Hill, 52–53
Columbus-Belmont Battlefield State Park, Columbus, 32
Cumberland Falls State Resort Park, Corbin, 88–89
Daniel Boone National Forest, Morehead, 58, 59
Fort Boonesborough State Park, Richmond, 83–84
General Butler State Resort Park, Carrollton, 5
Greenbo Lake State Park, Greenup, 54–55
Jenny Wiley State Resort Park, Prestonsburg, 128

John James Audubon State Park, Henderson, 23
Kenlake State Resort Park, Hardin, 35
Kentucky Dam Village State Resort Park, Gilbertsville, 36
Lake Barkley State Resort Park, Cadiz, 63
Lincoln Homestead Golf Course, Springfield, 107
Mammoth Cave National Park, Cave City, 73–74
Natural Bridge State Resort Park, Slade, 120–122
Pennyrile State Forest Resort Park, Dawson Springs, 36–37
Pine Mountain State Resort Park, Pineville, 135–136
Red River Gorge Geological Area, Nada, 122–123
Shakertown, Pleasant Hill, 101–102

PARKS and WILDLIFE
Ballard County Wildlife Management Area, Oscar, 30–31
Big Bone Lick State Park, Union, 2
Big South Fork National River and Recreation Area, Blue Heron, 89–90
Blue Licks Battlefield State Park, Blue Licks, 93–95
Breaks Interstate Park, Breaks, Virginia, 130–132
Buckhorn Lake State Resort Park, Buckhorn, 124–125

PARKS and WILDLIFE (*cont.*)
Carter Caves State Resort
 Park, Olive Hill, 52–53
Central Park, Ashland, 58
Central Park, Henderson, 24
Central Park, Louisville, 15
Cherokee Park, Louisville,
 15
Columbus-Belmont
 Battlefield State Park,
 Columbus, 31, 32
Creason Park, Louisville, 15
Cumberland Falls State
 Resort Park, Corbin, 88–89
Cumberland Gap National
 Historical Park, 137
Fountain Square, Bowling
 Green, 71
General Butler State Resort
 Park, Carrollton, 5–6
Greenbo Lake State Park,
 Greenup, 53–55
Jenny Wiley State Resort
 Park, Prestonsburg,
 128–129
Jesse Stuart State Nature
 Preserve, W-Hollow, 55
John James Audubon State
 Park, Henderson, 23
Kenlake State Resort Park,
 Hardin, 35
Kentucky Dam Village State
 Resort Park, Gilbertsville,
 36
Kentucky Horse Park,
 Lexington, 81–82
Lake Barkley State Resort
 Park, Cadiz, 63
Lilley Cornett Woods,
 Skyline, 133–134
Mammoth Cave National

Park, Cave City, 71–74
My Old Kentucky Home
 State Park, Bardstown,
 112–113
Natural Bridge State Resort
 Park, Slade, 120–122
Old Fort Harrod State Park,
 Harrodsburg, 103–104
Otter Creek Park, Rock
 Haven, 20
Pennyrile State Forest Resort
 Park, Dawson Springs,
 36–37
Pilot Knob State Nature
 Preserve, Clay City,
 119–120
Pine Mountain's Nature
 Preserve, Pineville, 135
Pine Mountain State Resort
 Park, Pineville, 135–136
Round Table Literary Park,
 Hopkinsville, 64
Seneca Park, Louisville, 15
Trail of Tears
 Commemorative Park,
 Hopkinsville, 65–66
Woodlands Nature Center,
 Land Between the Lakes, 42
PLANETARIUMS. See
 GALLERIES, MUSEUMS
 and PLANETARIUMS

RESTAURANTS
Afro-German Tea Room,
 Louisville, 14–15
Beehive Tavern, Augusta, 46
Caproni's, Maysville, 49
Carrollton Inn, Carrollton, 6
Chimney Corner Tea Room,
 Ashland, 58

Courthouse Cafe,
Whitesburg, 133
Creek's Drugstore, Harlan,
134
Crockett's Restaurant,
Hopkinsville, 64
Depot, Midway, 82, 99
Dietrich's in the Crescent,
Louisville, 14
Down Under, Richmond, 85
Elmwood Inn, Perryville,
105
Erhmann's Bakery,
Louisville, 15
General Butler State Resort
Park, Carrollton, 5
Harlan Sanders Cafe &
Museum, Corbin, 87–88,
137–138
Holbrook Drugstore,
Morehead, 58–59
Horseman's Fodder Cafe,
Midway, 82–83, 99
Jack Fry's, Louisville, 14
Jay's Sandwich Shop,
Harlan, 135
Kaelin's, Louisville, 14
Kentucky Fried Chicken,
Corbin, 87–88, 138
Kunz's Fourth & Market,
Louisville, 14
La Paloma, Louisville, 14
Lilly's, Louisville, 14
Patti's 1880 restaurant,
Grand Rivers, 41
Pendennis Club, Louisville,
13
Purple Cow, Beattyville,
123
Rudyard Kipling, Louisville,
14

Shakertown, Pleasant Hill,
102
Snowball Dining Room,
Cave City, 73–74
South Forks restaurant,
Elkton, 67
Thomason's, Henderson, 23
Vincenzo's, Louisville, 14
Woody's, Richmond, 85
RETREATS. See CHURCHES,
MONASTERIES,
RETREATS and SHRINES
RIVERS. See CREEKS,
LAKES, RIVERS and
SPRINGS

SCHOOLS. See COLLEGES,
SCHOOLS and
UNIVERSITIES
SHOPS. See ANTIQUES,
CRAFTS and GIFT SHOPS
SHRINES. See CHURCHES,
MONASTERIES,
RETREATS and SHRINES
SIDE TRIPS and TRAVELS
Buffalo Trace, 92–93
Cynthiana, 95–96
Danville, 105
Georgetown, 98–99
Hardinsburg to Hawesville,
21–22
Hazel, 34–35
Kentucky Horse Park,
Lexington, 81–82, 97
Mary Ingles Trail, 51
Midway, 99–100
Mount Sterling to
Owingsville, 119
Rabbit Hash, 2–4
Sheltowee Trace Trail, 59

SIDE TRIPS and TRAVELS
(cont.)
Smith's Wagon Road. See
Buffalo Trace
The Trace, 42
Zilpo Scenic Byway, 59
SPECIAL EVENTS
Arts and Crafts Festival,
Augusta, 47
Battle of Blue Licks
reenactment, Blue Licks, 94
Battle of Perryville
reenactment, Perryville,
106
Black Gold Festival, Hazard,
126
Blue Grass Stakes,
Keeneland, 82
Bourbon County Fair and
Saddlehorse Show, Paris,
97
Carter Caves Crawlathon,
Olive Hill, 53
Celebration of Traditional
Music Festival, Berea, 86
Corn Island Storytelling
Festival, Louisville, 16
Court Day, Mount Sterling,
119
Dickens on Main Street,
Louisville, 16
Dinsmore Homestead
Christmas party,
Burlington, 80
Dinsmore Homestead
Harvest Festival,
Burlington, 80
Dogwood Festival, Paducah,
26
Founder's Day, Salyersville,
128

Frontier Christmas,
Washington, 51
Gospel Song Festival,
Breaks, 131
Great American Brass Band
Festival, Danville, 105
Great American Dulcimer
Convention, Pineville, 135
Hard Scuffle Steeplechase,
Prospect, 16
Hazel Day, Hazel, 34–35
Hillbilly Days Festival,
Pikeville, 130
Humana Festival of New
American Plays,
Louisville, 16
Jesse Stuart weekend,
Greenup, 54
Kentucky Corps of
Longriflemen Interstate
Invitational Tournament,
Richmond, 84
Kentucky Derby Festival,
Louisville, 16
Kentucky Guild of Artists
and Craftsmen Fair, Berea,
86
Kentucky Highlands Folk
Festival, Prestonsburg, 129
Kentucky Scottish Weekend,
Carrollton, 5
Kentucky Shakespeare
Festival, Louisville, 15
Light Up Louisville,
Louisville, 16
Logan County Tobacco
Festival, Russellville, 68
Louisville City Fair,
Louisville, 16
Mountain Laurel Festival,
Pineville, 135

Mushroom Foray, Slade, 121
Nature Photography
    Shootout Weekend,
    Corbin, 89
Old Christmas celebration,
    Prestonsburg, 129
Old Reliable Germantown
    Fair and Horse Show,
    Germantown, 47
Picnic, Fancy Farm, 35
Poke Sallit Festival, Harlan,
    134–135
Purchase District Fair,
    Mayfield, 35
Quilt Festival, Paducah,
    25–26
Seedtime on the
    Cumberland, Whitesburg,
    133
Spring Craft Fair, Buckhorn,
    124
Square Dance and Clogging
    Festival, Slade, 121
St. Patrick's Square Dance,
    Prestonsburg, 129
Sternwheeler Regatta,
    Augusta, 47
Trail of Tears Intertribal
    Indian Pow Wow,
    Hopkinsville, 66
Trigg County Ham Festival,
    Cadiz, 63
White Hall antique car show,
    Richmond, 84
White Hall concert,
    Richmond, 84
Wildflower weekend, Slade,
    121
World Coon Hunter
    Championship, Mayfield,
    35

SPRINGS. See CREEKS,
    LAKES, RIVERS and
    SPRINGS
STATUES. See HISTORIC
    SITES and STATUES

THEATERS
    Actors Theater, Louisville,
        10, 13, 16
    Bailey's Country Store Radio
        Show, Williamsburg, 91
    Horse Cave Theater, Horse
        Cave, 74
    Jenny Wiley Theater,
        Prestonsburg, 128
    Kentucky Center for the
        Arts, Louisville, 10, 13
    Louisville Bach Society,
        Louisville, 10
    Louisville Ballet, Louisville, 10
    Louisville Orchestra,
        Louisville, 10
    Market House theater,
        Paducah, 26
    My Old Kentucky Home
        State Park, Bardstown,
        112–113
    Paramount Arts Center,
        Ashland, 58
TOURISM and
    INFORMATION
    CENTERS
    Gladie Cabin, Nada, 122
    Maysville-Mason County
        Tourism Commission,
        Maysville, 49
    Richmond Tourism Center,
        Richmond, 85
    Visitors Information Center,
        Carrollton, 6

TOURISM and
  INFORMATION
  CENTERS (*cont.*)
  Welcome Center, Berea, 85–86
  Welcome Center,
  Henderson, 23–24
TOWNS. See CITIES and
  TOWNS
TRAINS
  Big South Fork Scenic
  Railway, Stearns, 89, 90
  My Old Kentucky Home
  Dinner Train, Bardstown,
  112
TRAVELS. See SIDE TRIPS and
  TRAVELS

UNIVERSITIES. See
  COLLEGES, SCHOOLS
  and UNIVERSITIES

WAR SITES and CEMETERIES
  Battle site, Richmond, 85
  Blue Licks Battlefield State
  Park, Blue Licks, 93–95
  Buckner Homestead,
  Brandenburg, 21
  Cave Hill Cemetery,
  Louisville, 15
  Central Park, Henderson, 24
  Columbus-Belmont
  Battlefield State Park,
  Columbus, 31, 32
  Maplewood Cemetery,
  Mayfield, 35–36
  Morgan's Raiders, Midway,
  100
  Night Riders War site,
  Hopkinsville, 64–65

Perryville Battlefield State
  Historic Site, Perryville,
  101, 105–106
WELL-KNOWN PEOPLE
  Abraham Lincoln, 20, 22, 66,
  103, 107–108
  Al Capone, 40
  Carry Nation, 87
  Casey Jones, 33
  Charles Dickens, 9
  Charles Lindbergh, 73
  Colonel Harlan Sanders, 15,
  137–138
  Daniel Boone, 20, 49, 55–56,
  59, 83–84, 94, 96, 103, 120,
  123–124, 136–137
  Edgar Cayce, 65
  Franklin Gary Powers, 133
  Harriet Beecher Stowe, 22
  Herbert Hoover, 11
  Jefferson Davis, 66
  Jesse James, 20, 68
  Jesse Stuart, 54, 55, 56
  John James Audubon, 23
  John Muir, 75
  Josiah Henson, 22–23
  Loretta Lynn, 129
  Mark Twain, 33–34
  Mike Finn, 6–7
  Patrick Henry, 20
  Robert Penn Warren, 67
  Rosemary Clooney, 46
  Stephen Foster, 112–113
  Theodore Roosevelt, 80
  Thomas Jefferson, 2, 9
  Thomas Merton, 110–111
  Wynonna Judd, 57
WILDLIFE. See PARKS and
  WILDLIFE

Other titles in the Country Roads Series:

Country Roads of Michigan
Country Roads of Massachusetts
Country Roads of Illinois
Country Roads of New Hampshire
Country Roads of Oregon
Country Roads of New York State
Country Roads of Indiana
Country Roads of Ohio
Country Roads of Vermont
Country Roads of Hawaii
Country Roads of Quebec
Country Days in New York City

All books are $9.95 at bookstores.
Or order directly from the publisher (add $3.00
shipping & handling for direct orders):

Country Roads Press
P.O. Box 286
Castine, Maine 04421
Toll-free phone number: **800-729-9179**